TEN TIMES BETTER
FREEDOM LIFE YOUTH STUDY

PROPHETESS M.P. WASHINGTON

A LIFE RESTORED

E	E	E	N	F	L	R	E	E	A	G	E	E	E
V	W	R	F	R	A	I	A	R	R	A	P	I	D
L	F	R	E	R	D	T	G	R	T	I	T	G	I
E	U	R	V	F	D	R	H	D	E	V	D	F	A
W	T	E	E	L	M	E	E	E	T	R	V	A	R
T	E	A	H	A	O	R	R	A	R	E	P	N	F
L	N	L	A	L	T	H	E	T	E	T	B	L	A
M	T	A	L	D	H	D	H	H	E	H	E	J	E
A	E	E	O	F	E	E	A	S	A	G	L	P	I
A	F	E	N	L	R	T	E	L	P	U	I	I	E
A	D	G	F	J	A	I	R	U	S	A	E	W	F
E	P	E	T	L	E	E	T	B	W	D	V	L	U
D	W	E	E	P	I	N	G	L	L	E	E	W	M
I	A	I	L	I	I	P	E	T	E	R	O	E	D

AFRAID
MOTHER
FATHER
DEATH
WEEPING
DAUGHTER
TWELVE
PETER
JAIRUS
FELL
BELIEVE

EVERYONE HAS TO FOLLOW THE LAWS AND RULES. SIN IS A BREAKING OF GOD'S LAW OF RIGHTEOUSNESS.

GOD DOES NOT PUNISH PEOPLE SIN DOES. IT IS LIKE IF YOU STICK YOUR HAND IN A FIRE, YOU WILL GET BURNT. GOD DOES NOT BURN YOU, THE DECISION TO STICK YOUR HAND IN THE FIRE WAS YOUR CHOICE.

SIN IS YOUR CHOICE. BUT KNOW TO LIE, TO STEAL, TO CHEAT ALL HAVE CONSEQUENCES.

SIN AND BAD DECISIONS CAN HURT YOUR LIFE. YOU MUST THINK FIRST ABOUT WHAT WILL HAPPEN TO YOU AFTER YOU MAKE YOUR DECISION TO DO WRONG!

MOST FAMOUS RAP & HIPHOP MUSIC ARTISTS

WHO WAS IT THAT SOLD THEIR SOUL?

Revelation 18:10-13

**9 And the kings of the earth, who have
committed fornication and lived
deliciously with her, shall bewail her, and
lament for her, when they shall see the
smoke of her burning, 10 Standing afar off
for the fear of her torment, saying, Alas,
alas that great city Babylon, that mighty
city! for in one hour is thy judgment come.
11 And the merchants of the earth shall
weep and mourn over her; for no man
buyeth their merchandise any more:
12 THE MERCHANDISE of gold, and silver,
and precious stones, and of pearls, and
fine linen, and purple, and silk, and
scarlet, and all thyine wood, and all
manner vessels of ivory, and all manner
vessels of most precious wood, and of
brass, and iron, and marble, 13 And
cinnamon, and odours, and ointments,
and frankincense, and wine, and oil, and
fine flour, and wheat, and beasts, and
sheep, and horses, and chariots, and
slaves, and SOULS OF MEN.**

TO SELL YOUR SOUL IS TO DO SOMTHEING THAT IS WRONG IN THE SIGHT OF GOD IN EXCHANGE FOR WEALTH, POWER OR PROSPERITY.

GOD CREATED EVERY SOUL FOR HIS GLORY. Why does the world want you to compromise your faith in order to buy your soul?

THESE ARE THE THINGS THAT I AM DEEPLY CONCERNED ABOUT.

TODAYS DATE:

THIS IS WHY WE KNOW WE ARE TEN TIMES BETTER!

DANIEL 1:17 As for these four children, God gave them knowledge and skill in all learning and wisdom: and Daniel had understanding in all visions and dreams.

18 Now at the end of the days that the king had said he should bring them in, then the prince of the eunuchs brought them in before Nebuchadnezzar.

19 And the king communed with them; and among them all was found none like Daniel, Hananiah, Mishael, and Azariah: therefore stood they before the king.

20 And in all matters of wisdom and understanding, that the king enquired of them, he found them ten times better than all the magicians and astrologers that were in all his realm.

SOME PEOPLE DO THINGS THAT THEY KNOW ARE NOT PLEASING TO GOD AND THEY STILL SAY THAT THEY ARE SAVED. BUT TO BE SAVED YOU HAVE TO BE OBEDIENT TO GOD. YOU MUST CHOOSE GOD'S WAY OVER WHAT IS POPULAR SOMETIMES. LIST THREE THINGS YOU MIGHT HAVE TO DO THAT MIGHT CAUSE YOU TO BE CRITICIZED BY THE WORLD:

1	
2	
3	

KNOWING AND CHOOSING GOD IS WHAT MAKES ME 10 X B

THE WORLD IS NOT THE EARTH. IT IS THE SYSTEMS THAT GOVERN ALL UNBELIEVERS. SOMETIMES IT SEEMS RIGHT. BUT A FRIEND TO THE WORLD IS AN ENEMY OF GOD.

James 4:4 Ye adulterers and adulteresses, know ye not that the friendship of the world is enmity with God? whosoever therefore will be a friend of the world is the enemy of God. THIS MEANS THAT YOU CANNOT DO WHAT THE WORLD DOES. YOU MUST DO WHAT THE LORD SAYS TO DO.

TEN TIMES BETTER!

WHAT FEELS LIKE FUN AND WHAT LOOKS LIKE FUN CAN SOMETIMES SCAR OR HURT YOUR FUTURE. LIST THREE THINGS THAT MIGHT LOOK LIKE FUN WITH YOUR FRIENDS BUT CAN HURT YOUR FUTURE:

1	
2	
3	

LEARN THE STORY OF THE FRIENDSHIP OF REHOBOAM AND JEROBOAM AND HOW FOLLOWING THE ADVICE OF A FRIEND JUST TO IMPRESS HIM ENDED UP HURT REHOBOAMS FUTURE

Rehoboam and Jeroboam were childhood friends and later in life they both ruled as kings of Israel.

Rehoboam was the son of Solomon. He ruled over Judah which was in the south. Jeroboam, his friend at one time worked for Solomon, and later became king of Israel in the north.

READ THE STORY AND UNDERLINE THE FACTS:

1 Kings 12:1 And Rehoboam went to Shechem: for all Israel were come to Shechem to make him king.

2 And it came to pass, when Jeroboam the son of Nebat, who was yet in Egypt, heard of it, (for he
was fled from the presence of king Solomon, and Jeroboam dwelt in Egypt;)

3 That they sent and called him. And Jeroboam and all the congregation of Israel came, and spake
unto Rehoboam, saying,

4 Thy father made our yoke grievous: now therefore make thou the grievous service of thy father, and his heavy yoke which he put upon us, lighter, and we will serve thee.

5 And he said unto them, Depart yet for three days, then come again to me. And the people departed.

6 And king Rehoboam consulted with the old men, that stood before Solomon his father while he yet lived, and said, How do ye advise that I may answer this people?

7 And they spake unto him, saying, If thou wilt be a servant unto this people this day, and wilt serve them, and answer them, and speak good words to them, then they will be thy servants for ever.

8 But he forsook the counsel of the old men, which they had given him, and consulted with the young men that were grown up with him, and which stood before him:

9 And he said unto them, What counsel give ye that we may answer this people, who have spoken to me, saying, Make the yoke which thy father did put upon us lighter?

10 And the young men that were grown up with him spake unto him, saying, Thus shalt thou speak unto this people that spake unto thee, saying, Thy father made our yoke heavy, but make thou it lighter unto us; thus shalt thou say unto them, My little finger shall be thicker than my father's loins.

11 And now whereas my father did lade you with a heavy yoke, I will add to your yoke: my father hath chastised you with whips, but I will chastise you with scorpions.

12 So Jeroboam and all the people came to Rehoboam the third day, as the king had appointed, saying, Come to me again the third day.

13 And the king answered the people roughly, and forsook the old men's counsel that they gave him;

14 And spake to them after the counsel of the young men, saying, My father made your yoke heavy, and I will add to your yoke: my father also chastised you with whips, but I will chastise you with scorpions.

[15] Wherefore the king hearkened not unto the people; for the cause was from the LORD, that he might perform his saying, which the LORD spake by Ahijah the Shilonite unto Jeroboam the son of Nebat.

[16] So when all Israel saw that the king hearkened not unto them, the people answered the king, saying, What portion have we in David? neither have we inheritance in the son of Jesse: to your tents, O Israel: now see to thine own house, David. So Israel departed unto their tents.

[17] But as for the children of Israel which dwelt in the cities of Judah, Rehoboam reigned over them.

WHY DO YOU THINK REHOBOAM LISTENED TO HIS FRIENDS AND NOT TO THE VOICE OF WISDOM FROM THE ELDERS?

WHAT DOES IT MEAN TO WALK TOGETHER?

Amos 3:3 Can two walk together, except they be agreed?

WHAT IS GOD TEACHING REGARDING WHO YOU CHOOSE TO BE YOUR FRIEND IN AMOS 3:3?

LIFE IS ALWAYS ABOUT CHANGE. YOU ARE A SPIRIT THEREFORE YOU ARE ALWAYS CHANGING. SOMETIMES YOU CAN CHANGE AND NOT BE AWARE THAT YOU HAVE CHANGED.

THINK OF WHAT YOU EXPOSE YOURSELF TO AT HOME AND AT SCHOOL, MUSIC AND EVEN AMONG FAMILY WHAT AREA OR WHOULD

WOULD YOU SAY INFLUENCES YOU THE MOST?

____

____

WHY?

____

____

1 Corinthians 6:[19] What? know ye not that your body is the temple of the Holy Ghost which is in you, which ye have of God, and ye are not your own?

In the Old Testament Adam sinned against God, and this sin caused him to have to separate from God. God is holy and He does not dwell where there is sin. Therefore, Adam could not fellowship with God anymore. But he needed to be able to fellowship with God because God is man's source of life. Since Adam sinned, all of his children after him sinned.

Adam and Eve

Romans 6:23
For the wages of sin is death; but the gift of God is eternal life THROUGH JESUS CHRIST OUR LORD.

Understand this was the law at that time:
Exodus 21:24 "Eye for eye, tooth for tooth, hand for hand, foot for foot,".

If you took an eye you had to give an________

If you took a tooth you had to give a________

If you took a hand you had to give a ________

If you took a foot you had to give a ________________________________.

If you took a life you had to give a ____________________________ .

Since man gave up his life with God because of sin, he needed a sinless life to atone, which means to please God so that God would return and live again in him.

MAN DID NOT HAVE A SINLESS LIFE TO GIVE.

THIS IS WHY THEY BEGIN TO SACRIFICE THE LIFE OF LAMB.

YOUR LIFE IS IN YOUR BLOOD. IF YOU LOSE YOUR BLOOD, THEN YOU WILL DIE.

1 Corinthians 6:[19] What? know ye not that your body is the temple of the Holy Ghost which is in you, which ye have of God, and ye are not your own?

The blood of the lamb was a substitute for a person's blood because he was in sin, and sin is what causes man to die.

IT WAS THE SINS OF MAN'S THAT CAUSED HIS LIFE WAS SEPARATED FROM GOD.

THEREFORE, A LIFE HAD TO BE GIVEN BACK. THE LIFE OF SINLESS JESUS THE LAMB OF GOD THAT HAD TO BE GIVEN IN THE PLACE OF YOUR OWN.

REMEMEBER:

EXODUS 21:24 EYE FOR EYE, TOOTH FOR TOOTH, HAND FOR HAND, FOOT FOR FOOT

1 Corinthians 6:[20] For ye are bought with a price: therefore glorify God in your body, and in your sp rit, which are God's.

A LAMB WAS SLAN BECAUSE A LAMB IS EASILY LEAD ASTRAY. THOSE WHO PRACTICE SIN DO NOT KNOW THAT ARE DYING.

If you took an eye you had to give

an________If you took a tooth you had to give a_________If you took a hand you had to give a _________If you took a foot you had to give a

IF SIN TOOK A LIFE, WHAT HAD TO BE GIVEN IN ITS PLACE?

You live because you have blood.

YOU NEED BLOOD. IF YOU TOOK THE LIFE THAT WAS IN THE BLOOD THEN YOU HAVE TO GIVE BACK A LIFE OR SHED BLOOD.

It was blood of JESUS that paid the penalty for sin.

YOUR BODY IS A TABERNACLE FOR GOD. IT HOLDS YOUR SOUL, YOUR SPIRIT AND THE SPIRIT OF GOD.

WHEN YOUR BLOOD IS SPILLED, YOUR LIFE IS GONE OUT OF YOUR FLESH. THAT MEANS YOUR SOUL IS GONE. YOUR SPIRIT IS GONE, AND YOUR FLESH IS DEAD.

1 Corinthians 6:[19] What? know ye not that your body is the temple of the Holy Ghost which is in you, which ye have of God, and ye are not your own?

NOW TELL WHY DO YOU NEED BLOOD TO LIVE IN THE EARTH

____

Leviticus 17:11 For the life of the flesh is in the blood: and I have given it to you upon the altar to make an atonement for your souls: for it is the blood that maketh an atonement for the soul.

WHERE IS YOUR LIFE?

____

NOW TELL WHY DO YOU HAVE TO GIVE BLOOD TO ATONE WHICH MEANS TO PLEASE GOD?

____

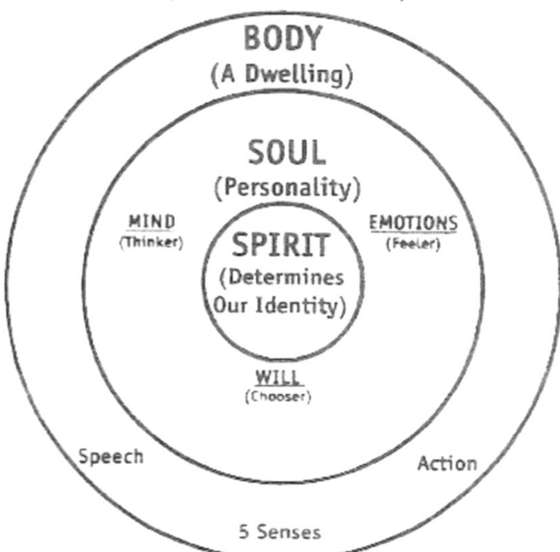

THIS OFFERING OF THE LAMBS BLOOD IS WHAT WAS USED TO GIVE A LIFE FOR THE LIFE THAT MAN HAD TAKEN FROM GOD. THIS BLOOD IS WHAT WE CALL SAVING BLOOD.

WHAT IS THIS BLOOD CALLED?

____

The problem was each time a lamb was sacrificed, men kept on sinning. This is why the blood of the lamb was not able to save man. Mankind needed the Blood of God. God sent His Son, and His Son Jesus became the Sacrificial Lamb. He came to FULFILL THE LAW- a LIFE FOR a LIFE. He gave a sinless life in exchange for your sinful life.

1 Corinthians 6:[19] What? know ye not that your body is the temple of the Holy Ghost which is in you, which ye have of God, and ye are not your own?

John 1: [26] John answered them, saying, I baptize with water: but there standeth one among you,
whom ye know not; [27] He it is, who coming after me is preferred before me, whose shoe's latchet I
am not worthy to unloose.

[28] These things were done in Bethabara beyond
Jordan, where John was baptizing.

[29] The next day John seeth Jesus coming unto him,
and saith, Behold the Lamb of God, which taketh
away the sin of the world

WHAT WAS JESUS CALLED?

____

WHY WAS JESUS CALLED THE LAMB OF GOD? ______________________________

____

____

John 1:29-32. The next day John seeth Jesus coming unto him, and saith, Behold the Lamb of God, which taketh away the sin of the world.

WHAT DID JESUS COME TO DO?

____

____

DID JESUS HAVE TO DIE AS A SACRIFICIAL LAMB TO TAKE AWAY YOU'RE SINS?

EXPLAIN HOW JESUS BECAME THE LAMB OF GOD

____

____

____

1 Corinthians 6:19 What? know ye not that your body is the temple of the Holy Ghost which is in you, which ye have of God, and ye are not your own?

1 John 1:7 But if we walk in the light, as he is in the light, we have fellowship one with another, and the blood of Jesus Christ his Son cleanseth us from all sin.

YOUR LIFE IS IN YOUR BLOOD AND THE BLOOD OF JESUS CONTAINS THE LIFE OF JESUS. HIS BLOOD WAS SHED ON THE CROSS JUST LIKE A LAMB. GOD MADE HIS LIFE THE WORD OF GOD.

WHAT DOES THE BLOOD OF JESUS DO FOR US?

Three very important words:

1. **SALVATION**
2. **RECONCILIATION**
3. **REDEEMED**

THIS IS WHAT I LEARNED ABOUT THE NEED FOR THE BLOOD OF A LAMB :

____
____
____
____

SALVATION - TO RESCUE OR TO DELIVER

INCE I UNDERSTAND ABOUT THE BLOOD OF A LAMB NOW I AM

ROMANS 10: 8 But what saith it? The word is nigh thee, even in thy mouth, and in thy heart: that is,
the word of faith, which we preach; 9 That if thou shalt confess with thy mouth the Lord Jesus, and
shalt believe in thine heart that God hath raised him from the dead, THOU SHALT BE SAVED.

10 For with the heart man believeth unto righteousness; and with the mouth confession is made
unto salvation. 11 For the scripture saith, Whosoever believeth on him shall not be ashamed. 12 For

1 Corinthians 6:[19] What? know ye not that your body is the temple of the Holy Ghost which is in you, which ye have of God, and ye are not your own?

there is no difference between the Jew and the Greek: for the same Lord over all is rich unto all that call upon him. [13] For whosoever shall call upon the name of the Lord shall be saved.

WHAT MUST YOU DO TO BECOME SAVED?

MY PRAYER OF SALVATION

Pray this aloud: "Lord Jesus, I CONFESS with my mouth that I believe in the Lord Jesus, and I believe in my heart that you raised Him from the dead. Today I accept Jesus as my Lord and Savior. Today I am saved.

FINISH THIS STATEMENT:
NOW THAT I AM SAVED I AM

RECONCILIATION

TO RESTORE OR TO BRING BACK2

Corinthians 5:[17] Therefore if any man be in Christ, he is a new creature: old things are passed away; behold, all things are become new.
[18] And
all things are of God, who hath RECONCILED US TO
HIMSELF BY JESUS CHRIST, and hath given to us the
ministry of reconciliation; [19] To wit, that GOD WAS IN
CHRIST, reconciling the world unto himself, not imputing
their trespasses unto them; and hath
committed unto us the word of reconciliation.

Going to Church

HOW DO YOU KNOW THAT YOU ARE CHANGED AND A NEW CREATURE?

WHAT DOES IT MEAN TO BE RECONCILED BACK TO GOD?

1 Corinthians 6:[19] What? know ye not that your body is the temple of the Holy Ghost which is in you, which ye have of God, and ye are not your own?

WHOSE BLOOD WAS IT THAT CAUSED YOU TO BE RECONCILED BACK TO GOD?

<u>DRAW THREE PICTURES</u> ONE OF A ANIMAL LAMB THE SINFUL MAN AND JESUS ON THE CROSS

THE ANIMAL LAMB	THE SINFUL MAN	THE LAMB OF GOD

Ephesians 2:[8] For by GRACE ARE YE SAVED through faith; and that not of yourselves: it is the gift of God:[9] Not of works, lest any man should boast.

REDEEMED

MEANS TO BE FREED OR RELEASED

Psalm 107:2 Let the redeemed of the LORD say so, whom he hath <u>redeemed from the hand of the enemy;</u>

YOU HAVE BEEN REDEEMED. THIS MEANS THAT YOU NOW HAVE A SAVIOR. THEREFORE, YOU HAVE A CHOICE IN WHO AND WHAT YOU WILL BE.

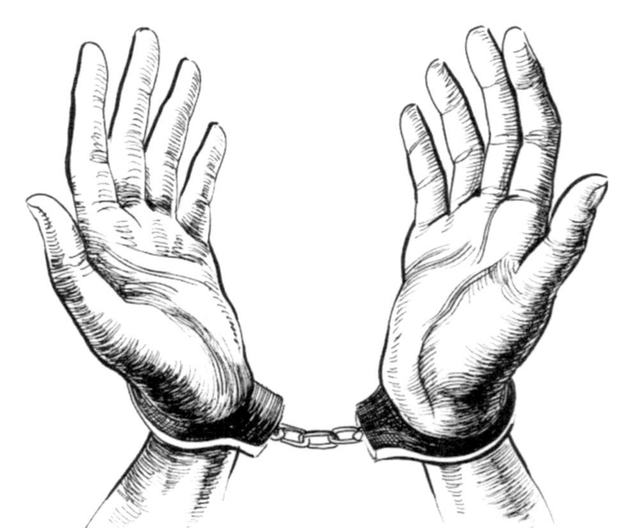

<u>MEN CONTINUED TO SIN</u> IN THE WORLD UNTIL GOD SENT HIS SON JESUS AND JESUS'S BLOOD SACRIFICE BROUGHT SALVATION.

NOW IT IS TIME TO GO BACK AND LOOK OVER YOUR NOTES, AND IN YOUR OWN WORDS TELL THE STORY OF SALVATION:

1 Corinthians 6:[19] What? know ye not that your body is the temple of the Holy Ghost which is in you, which ye have of God, and ye are not your own?

JESUS SAID: I am the light of the world:
(John 8:12)

IS HE LIGHT OR DARK?

If darkness is sin in the mind, how important is it to have a light?

I UNDERSTAND WHAT LIGHT IS AND I UNDERSTAND DARKNESS. I KNOW THAT I AM...

Ephesians 5:[8] For ye were sometimes darkness, but now are ye light in the Lord: walk as children of light:

SIN MEANS THAT YOUR THINKING IS OPPOSITE THE WORD OF GOD. YOU HAVE WRONG THOUGHS AND WRONG THOUGHTS MAKE BAD ACTIONS. THIS IS WHY SIN IS DARKNESS IN THE MIND AND THE WORD OF GOD IS LIGHT.

Psalm 119:[130] The entrance of thy words giveth light; it giveth understanding unto the simple.

WHEN A PERSON IS NOT SAVED, HIS OR HER IDEAS ARE CALLED DARK. WHEN A PERSON IS NOT SAVED, THEY MAKE A LOT OF MISTAKES IN LIFE BECAUSE THEIR THOUGHTS ARE IN THE DARK.

1 Corinthians 6:19 What? know ye not that your body is the temple of the Holy Ghost which is in you, which ye have of God, and ye are not your own?

LIST THREE WAYS YOU CAN KNOW IF SOMEONE IS
IN THE DARK AND NOT IN THE LIGHT.

1	
2	
3	

Colossians 1:13 Who hath delivered us from the power of darkness, and hath translated us into the kingdom of his dear Son:

WRITE THE A B C'S OF PRAISE

Choose a word each day to praise God that begins with the alphabet.
USE THIS FOR AN EXAMPLE BUT KEEP THE ALPHABETS IN ORDER!

YOU NEED TO BE SO FAMILIAR WITH PRAISE WORDS OR PHRASES THAT YOU CAN DO IT WITHOUT LOOKING.

EXAMPLE OF A PHRASE PRAISE: A IS FOR MY GOD ALWAYSS HELPS ME

1 Corinthians 6:[19] What? know ye not that your body is the temple of the Holy Ghost which is in you, which ye have of God, and ye are not your own?

A is for My God ALWAYS HELPS ME	N
B	O
C	P
D	Q
E	R
F	S
G	T
H	U
I	V
J	W
K	X
L	Y
M	Z

1 Corinthians 6:[19] What? know ye not that your body is the temple of the Holy Ghost which is in you, which ye have of God, and ye are not your own?

ALL ABOUT ME

I AM HAPPY WHEN...

My Most Important accomplishment.

ONE OF THE GREATEST THINGS I HAVE LEARNED IS...

My Future Goals for the next year.

1.
2.
3.
4.

MY BEST SKILL.

How I changed FROM last year

1 Corinthians 6:[19] What? know ye not that your body is the temple of the Holy Ghost which is in you, which ye have of God, and ye are not your own?

My Productive Daily Routine: Outline your ideal daily routine.

MORNING	NOON	EVENING	NIGHT

This is what I do when I am sad or discouraged:

MY FAVORITE FOODS ARE:

THE BEST ADVICE I CAN GIVE SOMEONE UNSAVED IS…

THESE ARE THE PEOPLE WHO ARE CLOSEST TO ME:

I KNOW I AM AT MY BEST WHEN…

1 Corinthians 6:[19] What? know ye not that your body is the temple of the Holy Ghost which is in you, which ye have of God, and ye are not your own?

THIS IS WHAT I WOULD LIKE TO LEARN:

Places I hope to visit:

THINGS THAT I MUST STOP BEING AFRAID OF:

If someone cares about me then they should…

My favorite Books and Movies are:

1 Corinthians 6:19 What? know ye not that your body is the temple of the Holy Ghost which is in you, which ye have of God, and ye are not your own?

What is the most important lesson life has taught you?

Two things I love about school:

I KNOW THAT GOD IS REAL BECAUSE…

The greatest challenge in my today life is:

THE TWO PEOPLE THAT I TURN TO WHEN I NEED HELP:

I KNOW THAT I AM GROWING UP BECAUSE…

eggs	larva	pupa	butterfly

UNTIL HE GROWS HIS WINGS

1 Corinthians 6:[19] What? know ye not that your body is the temple of the Holy Ghost which is in you, which ye have of God, and ye are not your own?

WHAT DO YOU HAVE TO DO TO KEEP YOUR LIFE SAFE?

I HAVE A RIGHT TO GROW IN PEACE AND IN THE BEAUTY OF THE LORD. BECAUSE I AM____

____

____

911 IS THE NUMBER I DAIL WHEN SOMEONE IS TRYING TO HURT ME.
NO ONE HAS A RIGHT TO HURT ME!

Proverbs 9:11 For by me thy days shall be multiplied, and the years of thy life shall be increased.

Romans 12:1 I beseech you therefore, brethren, by the mercies of God, that ye present your bodies a living sacrifice, holy, acceptable unto God, which is your reasonable service.

**THIS IS MY BODY
NO ONE HAS A RIGHT TO TOUCH ITNO ONE HAS A RIGHT TO HURT IT MY BODY BELONGS TO ME**

1 Corinthians 6:[19] What? know ye not that your body is the temple of the Holy Ghost which is in you, which ye have of God, and ye are not your own?

Romans 12:1 I beseech you therefore, brethren, by the mercies of God, that ye present your bodies a living sacrifice, holy, acceptable unto God, which is your reasonable service.

THIS IS HOW I SACRIFICE MY BODY UNTO GOD.

1 Corinthians 6:[19] What? know ye not that your body is the temple of the Holy Ghost which is in you, which ye have of God, and ye are not your own?

MY TEAM THIS YEAR TO MAKE MY LIFE BETTER:

MY CLOSEST FRIEND	
MY ADULT ADVISER	
WHO WILL HELP ME	
MY PRAYER PARTNER	
FINANCIAL HELP	
MY RIDE I CAN CALL ON	
WHO WILL COME AND SEE ABOUT ME	

THIS IS MY SUMMARY OF WHO I AM NOW

THIS IS THE SUMMARY OF WHOM I WILL GROW UP TO BECOME

1 Corinthians 6:[19] **What? know ye not that your body is the temple of the Holy Ghost which is in you, which ye have of God, and ye are not your own?**

Things about last year.

ONE SMART THING I DID	ONE DUMB THING	ONE THING I MUST WORK ON
ONE THING I WILL NEVER DO AGAIN	PEOPLE I MET	PEOPLE I NEED TO LEAVE BEHIND
WHAT I ACCOMPLISHED	HOW MUCH TIME DID I WASTE	MY GREATEST CHALLENGE
MY GREATEST SUCCESS		

1 Corinthians 6:[19] What? know ye not that your body is the temple of the Holy Ghost which is in you, which ye have of God, and ye are not your own?

WORDS TO DESCRIBE PERSONALITY TRAITS

1. humble
marked by meekness or modesty; not arrogant or prideful

2. brave
possessing or displaying courage

3. courageous
able to face and deal with danger or fear without flinching

4. serious
of great consequence

5. resourceful
adroit or imaginative

6. stubborn
tenaciously unwilling to yield

7. loyal
steadfast in allegiance or duty

8. gullible
naive and easily deceived or tricked

9. selfish
concerned chiefly with your own advantage

10. generous
willing to give and share unstintingly

11. self-confident
showing poise and assurance in your own worth

12. respectful
exhibiting an attitude of admiration or esteem

13. considerate
showing concern for the rights and feelings of others

14. imaginative
marked by independence and creativity in thought or action

15. brilliant
full of light; shining intensely

16. creative
having the ability or power to invent or make something

17. independent
free from external control and constraint

18. carefree
without trouble or worry

19. studious
characterized by diligent study and fondness for reading

20. intelligent
having the capacity for thought and reason to a high degree

21. honest
marked by truth

22. mischievous
naughtily or annoyingly playful

23. adventurous
willing to undertake new and daring enterprises

24. hardworking
characterized by hard work and perseverance

25. daring
a challenge to do something dangerous or foolhardy

26. charming
pleasing or delighting

27. lazy

disinclined to work or exertion

28. patriotic

inspired by love for your country

29. successful

having succeeded or being marked by a favorable outcome

30. responsible

worthy of or requiring trust; held accountable

31. helpful
providing assistance or serving a useful function

32. cautious

showing careful forethought

33. polite

showing regard for others in manners, speech, behavior, etc.

34. conceited

having an exaggerated sense of self-importance

35. leader

a person who rules or guides or inspires others

36. demanding

requiring more than usually expected or thought due

37. bossy

offensively self-assured or exercising unwarranted power

38. gentle

soft and mild; not harsh or stern or severe

39. loving

feeling or showing love and affection

40. proud

feeling self-respect, self-esteem, or self-importance

41. mysterious

beyond ordinary understanding

42. eager

having or showing keen interest or intense desire

43. hopeful

having or manifesting optimism

44. lucky

having or bringing good fortune

45. cooperative

involving the joint activity of two or more

46. ambitious

having a strong desire for success or achievement

47. quiet
characterized by an absence of agitation or activity

48. curious
eager to investigate and learn or learn more

49. mature
having reached full natural growth or development

50. witty
demonstrating striking cleverness and humor

51. determined
having been learned or found especially by investigation

52. energetic
possessing or displaying forceful exertion

53. rude
belonging to an early stage of technical development

54. strict
rigidly accurate; allowing no deviation from a standard

55. annoyed
troubled persistently

56. foolish
lacking good sense or judgment

57. grumpy
annoyed and irritable

58. miserable
very unhappy

59. talented
endowed with talent or talents

60. sly
marked by skill in deception

61. skillful
having or showing knowledge, ability, or aptitude

62. thoughtful
exhibiting or characterized by careful consideration

63. tolerant
showing or characterized by broad-mindedness

64. trustworthy
worthy of trust or belief

65. weak
wanting in physical strength

66. wise
having intelligence and discernment

67. jealous
suspicious or fearful of being displaced by a rival

68. lonely
lacking companions or companionship

69. timid
showing fear and lack of courage

70. shy
timid and lacking self-confide

1 Corinthians 6:[19] What? know ye not that your body is the temple of the Holy Ghost which is in you, which ye have of God, and ye are not your own?

NUMBERING MY FEELINGS FOR 180 DAYS

DAY	DAY	DAY	DAY	DAY	DAY	DAY
DAY	DAY	DAY	DAY	DAY	DAY	DAY
DAY	DAY	DAY	DAY	DAY	DAY	DAY
DAY	DAY	DAY	DAY	DAY	DAY	DAY
DAY	DAY	DAY	DAY	DAY	DAY	DAY
DAY	DAY	DAY	DAY	DAY	DAY	DAY
DAY	DAY	DAY	DAY	DAY	DAY	DAY
DAY	DAY	DAY	DAY	DAY	DAY	DAY
DAY	DAY	DAY	DAY	DAY	DAY	DAY
DAY	DAY	DAY	DAY	DAY	DAY	DAY
DAY	DAY	DAY	DAY	DAY	DAY	DAY
DAY	DAY	DAY	DAY	DAY	DAY	DAY

1 Corinthians 6:[19] What? know ye not that your body is the temple of the Holy Ghost which is in you, which ye have of God, and ye are not your own?

NUMBERING MY FEELINGS FOR 180 DAYS

DAY	DAY	DAY	DAY	DAY	DAY	DAY
DAY	DAY	DAY	DAY	DAY	DAY	DAY
DAY	DAY	DAY	DAY	DAY	DAY	DAY
DAY	DAY	DAY	DAY	DAY	DAY	DAY
DAY	DAY	DAY	DAY	DAY	DAY	DAY
DAY	DAY	DAY	DAY	DAY	DAY	DAY
DAY	DAY	DAY	DAY	DAY	DAY	DAY
DAY	DAY	DAY	DAY	DAY	DAY	DAY
DAY	DAY	DAY	DAY	DAY	DAY	DAY
DAY	DAY	DAY	DAY	DAY	DAY	DAY
DAY	DAY	DAY	DAY	DAY	DAY	DAY
DAY	DAY	DAY	DAY	DAY	DAY	DAY

1 Corinthians 6:[19] What? know ye not that your body is the temple of the Holy Ghost which is in you, which ye have of God, and ye are not your own?

THINGS I AM GRATEFUL FOR:

DAY	DAY	DAY	DAY	DAY	DAY	DAY
DAY	DAY	DAY	DAY	DAY	DAY	DAY
DAY	DAY	DAY	DAY	DAY	DAY	DAY
DAY	DAY	DAY	DAY	DAY	DAY	DAY
DAY	DAY	DAY	DAY	DAY	DAY	DAY
DAY	DAY	DAY	DAY	DAY	DAY	DAY
DAY	DAY	DAY	DAY	DAY	DAY	DAY
DAY	DAY	DAY	DAY	DAY	DAY	DAY
DAY	DAY	DAY	DAY	DAY	DAY	DAY
DAY	DAY	DAY	DAY	DAY	DAY	DAY
DAY	DAY	DAY	DAY	DAY	DAY	DAY
DAY	DAY	DAY	DAY	DAY	DAY	DAY

1 Corinthians 6:19 What? know ye not that your body is the temple of the Holy Ghost which is in you, which ye have of God, and ye are not your own?

THINGS I AM GRATEFUL FOR:

DAY	DAY	DAY	DAY	DAY	DAY	DAY
DAY	DAY	DAY	DAY	DAY	DAY	DAY
DAY	DAY	DAY	DAY	DAY	DAY	DAY
DAY	DAY	DAY	DAY	DAY	DAY	DAY
DAY	DAY	DAY	DAY	DAY	DAY	DAY
DAY	DAY	DAY	DAY	DAY	DAY	DAY
DAY	DAY	DAY	DAY	DAY	DAY	DAY
DAY	DAY	DAY	DAY	DAY	DAY	DAY
DAY	DAY	DAY	DAY	DAY	DAY	DAY
DAY	DAY	DAY	DAY	DAY	DAY	DAY
DAY	DAY	DAY	DAY	DAY	DAY	DAY
DAY	DAY	DAY	DAY	DAY	DAY	DAY

1 Corinthians 6:19 What? know ye not that your body is the temple of the Holy Ghost which is in you, which ye have of God, and ye are not your own?

PEEPING **WHAT'S UP AHEAD FOR MY LIFE**. THESE ARE THE GOALS I WANT TO ACCOMPLISH THIS YEAR

20___-20___

AUG.	SEPT.	OCT.	NOV.
DEC.	JAN.	FEB.	MAR.
APR.	MAY	JUNE	JULY

1 Corinthians 6:[19] What? know ye not that your body is the temple of the Holy Ghost which is in you, which ye have of God, and ye are not your own?

MY LIFE HAS A PURPOSE AND DESTINY

I MUST MAKE BETTER DECISIONS FOR ME BECAUSE MY CHOICES BUILDS MY OWN DESTINY

GOD HAS ASSIGNED ME A DESTINY. I MUST CHANGE SO THAT I CAN FIND MY DESTINY

I WILL KNOW MY DESTINY ONLY IF GOD RULES MY DECISIONS.

Five things about me that I need to improve

My weaknesses	My strengths

1 Corinthians 6:[19] What? know ye not that your body is the temple of the Holy Ghost which is in you, which ye have of God, and ye are not your own?

List five things a grown person should have if he or she is successful:

1	
2	
3	
4	
5	

ALL PATHS LEADS SOMEWHERE.

TELL WHERE A PATH WILL END UP.

A CHILD	WHEN HE IS GROWN
EXAMPLE: A CHILD WHO WILL NOT OBEY	THIS CHILD WILL END UP IN JAIL
A CHILD WHO HAS TROUBLE MAKERS FOR FRIENDS	
A CHILD WHO IS ALWAYS ANGRY	
A CHILD WHO FEELS UNLOVED	
A CHILD WHO FIGHTS ANYONE	
A CHILD HATES READING	
A CHILD WHO WILL NOT KEEP TRYING	
A CHILD WHO DOES NOT PRAY	
A CHILD WHO GIVES UP EASILY	
A CHILD WHO CURSES	
A CHILD WHO STEALS	
A CHILD WHO LIES	
A CHILD WHO WASTES TIME	

1 Corinthians 6:[19] What? know ye not that your body is the temple of the Holy Ghost which is in you, which ye have of God, and ye are not your own?

YOU ARE IN CONTROL OF YOUR PATH

NO MATTER WHAT PEOPLE DO TO YOU OR WHAT THEY SAY ABOUT YOU, ONE DAY YOU WILL GROW UP AND IF YOU ARE WISE, YOU WILL BECOME WHAT YOU CHOOSE TO BE, AND NOT WHAT OTHERS TRIED TO MAKE YOU BE. WRITE WHO AND WHAT WILL YOU BECOME?

USE THE TREES TO WRITE WHAT YOU SEE IN YOUR OWN FUTURE PATH.

USE THE PATH AND WRITE WHERE YOU ARE GOING!

#1 JESUS IS BORN!

Luke 2:1 And it came to pass in those days, that there went out a decree from Caesar Augustus that
all the world should be taxed.[2] (And this taxing was first made when Cyrenius was governor of
Syria.)[3] And all went to be taxed, every one into his own city.[4] And Joseph also went up from Galilee,
out of the city of Nazareth, into Judaea, unto the city of David, which is called Bethlehem; (because
he was of the house and lineage of David:)[5] To be taxed with Mary his espoused wife, being great
with child.[6] And so it was, that, while they were there, the days were accomplished that she should
be delivered.[7] And she brought forth her firstborn son, and wrapped him in swaddling clothes, and
laid him in a manger; because there was no room for them in the inn.[8] And there were in the same
country shepherds abiding in the field, keeping watch over their flock by night.[9] And, lo, the angel of
the Lord came upon them, and the glory of the Lord shone round about them: and they were sore
afraid.[10] And the angel said unto them, Fear not: for, behold, I bring you good tidings of great joy,
which shall be to all people.[11] For unto you is born this day in the city of David a Saviour, which is
Christ the Lord.[12] And this shall be a sign unto you; Ye shall find the babe wrapped in swaddling
clothes, lying in a manger.[13] And suddenly there was with the angel a multitude of the heavenly host
praising God, and saying,[14] Glory to God in the highest, and on earth peace, good will toward men.

1 Corinthians 6:[19] What? know ye not that your body is the temple of the Holy Ghost which is in you, which ye have of God, and ye are not your own?

When or where does this story take place?

List the characters:

Important Words

Is there a problem?

What was the plot or main idea?

Why is this story important?

How can knowing this help me?

1 Corinthians 6:[19] What? know ye not that your body is the temple of the Holy Ghost which is in you, which ye have of God, and ye are not your own?

TEN TIMES BETTER

L	T	T	F	C	A	M	E	L	E	R	S	E	N
I	I	A	O	L	T	N	N	I	S	I	A	I	O
T	C	N	L	A	O	O	B	I	O	M	T	C	I
L	A	D	I	F	S	G	O	E	L	N	N	E	T
L	N	O	F	S	E	C	G	A	E	E	F	S	A
F	I	F	E	R	S	I	M	M	I	T	O	A	I
L	B	I	L	F	O	J	E	T	T	T	E	L	L
I	L	A	A	A	A	N	O	L	H	S	J	V	I
O	O	I	M	L	O	I	N	T	C	L	E	A	C
N	O	E	B	T	O	T	T	A	A	N	S	T	N
G	D	C	A	G	R	N	V	H	O	U	U	I	O
F	R	A	C	B	E	A	E	L	E	E	S	O	C
D	O	R	S	M	E	C	C	N	E	E	I	N	E
M	E	G	R	N	E	I	O	O	T	S	N	B	R

GRACE
ATONEMENT
JESUS
LAMB
FAITH
LIFE
SIN
RECONCILIATION
BLOOD
SALVATION

1 Corinthians 6:19 What? know ye not that your body is the temple of the Holy Ghost which is in you, which ye have of God, and ye are not your own?

#2 THE ANGEL VISITS MARY

Luke 1:26 And in the sixth month the angel Gabriel was sent from God unto a city of Galilee, named Nazareth,27 To a
virgin espoused to a man whose name was Joseph, of the house of David; and the virgin's name was Mary.28 And the
angel came in unto her, and said, Hail, thou that art highly favoured, the Lord is with thee: blessed art thou among
women.29 And when she saw him, she was troubled at his saying, and cast in her mind what manner of salutation this
should be.30 And the angel said unto her, Fear not, Mary: for thou hast found favour with God.31 And, behold, thou shalt
conceive in thy womb, and bring forth a son, and shalt call his name JESUS.32 He shall be great, and shall be called the
Son of the Highest: and the Lord God shall give unto him the throne of his father David:33 And he shall reign over the
house of Jacob for ever; and of his kingdom there shall be no end.34 Then said Mary unto the angel, How shall this be,
seeing I know not a man?35 And the angel answered and said unto her, The Holy Ghost shall come upon thee, and the
power of the Highest shall overshadow thee: therefore also that holy thing which shall be born of thee shall be called
the Son of God.

1 Corinthians 6:[19] What? know ye not that your body is the temple of the Holy Ghost which is in you, which ye have of God, and ye are not your own?

When or where does this story take place?

List the characters:

Important Words

Is there a problem?

What was the plot or main idea?

Why is this story important?

How can knowing this help me?

1 Corinthians 6:[19] What? know ye not that your body is the temple of the Holy Ghost which is in you, which ye have of God, and ye are not your own?

A LIFE RESTORED

E	E	E	N	F	L	R	E	E	A	G	E	E	E
V	W	R	F	R	A	I	A	R	R	A	P	I	D
L	F	R	E	R	D	T	G	R	T	I	T	G	I
E	U	R	V	F	D	R	H	D	E	V	D	F	A
W	T	E	E	L	M	E	E	E	T	R	V	A	R
T	E	A	H	A	O	R	R	A	R	E	P	N	F
L	N	L	A	L	T	H	E	T	E	T	B	L	A
M	T	A	L	D	H	D	H	H	E	H	E	J	E
A	E	E	O	F	E	E	A	S	A	G	L	P	I
A	F	E	N	L	R	T	E	L	P	U	I	I	E
A	D	G	F	J	A	I	R	U	S	A	E	W	F
E	P	E	T	L	E	E	T	B	W	D	V	L	U
D	W	E	E	P	I	N	G	L	L	E	E	W	M
I	A	I	L	I	I	P	E	T	E	R	O	E	D

AFRAID
MOTHER
FATHER
DEATH
WEEPING
DAUGHTER
TWELVE
PETER
JAIRUS
FELL
BELIEVE

1 Corinthians 6:[19] What? know ye not that your body is the temple of the Holy Ghost which is in you, which ye have of God, and ye are not your own?

#3 JESUS HEALS JAIRUS DAUGHTER

Mark 5:22 And, behold, there cometh one of the rulers of the synagogue, Jairus by name; and when he saw him, he fell
at his feet, 23 And besought him greatly, saying, My little daughter lieth at the point of death: I pray thee, come and
lay thy hands on her, that she may be healed; and she shall live.24 And Jesus went with him; and much people followed
him, and thronged him25 And a certain woman,which had an issue of blood twelve years,26 And had suffered many
things of many physicians, and had spent all that she had, and was nothing bettered, but rather grew worse,27 When
she had heard of Jesus, came in the press behind, and touched his garment.28 For she said, If I may touch but his
clothes, I shall be whole.29 And straightway the fountain of her blood was dried up; and she felt in her body that she
was healed of that plague.30 And Jesus, immediately knowing in himself that virtue had gone out of him, turned him
about in the press, and said, Who touched my clothes?31 And his disciples said unto him, Thou seest the multitude
thronging thee, and sayest thou, Who touched me?32 And he looked round about to see her that had done this
thing.33 But the woman fearing and trembling, knowing what was done in her, came and fell down before him, and
told him all the truth.34 And he said unto her, Daughter, thy faith hath made thee whole; go in peace, and be whole of
thy plague.35 While he yet spake, there came from the ruler of the synagogue's house certain which said, Thy daughter
is dead: why troublest thou the Master any further?36 As soon as Jesus heard the word that was spoken, he saith unto
the ruler of the synagogue, Be not afraid, only believe.37 And he suffered no man to follow him, save Peter, and James,
and John the brother of James.38 And he cometh to the house of the ruler of the synagogue, and seeth the tumult,
and them that wept and wailed greatly.39 And when he was come in, he saith unto them, Why make ye this ado, and
weep? the damsel is not dead, but sleepeth.40 And they laughed him to scorn. But when he had put them all out, he
taketh the father and the mother of the damsel, and them that were with him, and entereth in where the damsel was
lying.41 And he took the damsel by the hand, and said unto her, Talitha cumi; which is, being interpreted, Damsel, I say
unto thee, arise.42 And straightway the damsel arose, and walked; for she was of the age of twelve years. And they
were astonished with a great astonishment. 43 And he charged them straitly that no man should know it; and
commanded that something should be given her to eat.

1 Corinthians 6:[19] What? know ye not that your body is the temple of the Holy Ghost which is in you, which ye have of God, and ye are not your own?

When or where does this story take place?

List the characters:

Important Words

Is there a problem?

What was the plot or main idea?

Why is this story important?

How can knowing this help me?

#4 JESUS TALKS TO A SAMARITAN WOMAN

John 4:[7] There cometh a woman of Samaria to draw water: Jesus saith unto her, Give me to drink.[8] (For his disciples
were gone away unto the city to buy meat.)[9] Then saith the woman of Samaria unto him, How is it that thou, being a
Jew, askest drink of me, which am a woman of Samaria? for the Jews have no dealings with the Samaritans.[10] Jesus
answered and said unto her, If thou knewest the gift of God, and who it is that saith to thee, Give me to drink; thou
wouldest have asked of him, and he would have given thee living water.[11] The woman saith unto him, Sir, thou hast
nothing to draw with, and the well is deep: from whence then hast thou that living water?[12] Art thou greater than our
father Jacob, which gave us the well, and drank thereof himself, and his children, and his cattle?[13] Jesus answered and
said unto her, Whosoever drinketh of this water shall thirst again:[14] But whosoever drinketh of the water that I shall give
him shall never thirst; but the water that I shall give him shall be in him a well of water springing up into everlasting
life.[15] The woman saith unto him, Sir, give me this water, that I thirst not, neither come hither to draw.[16] Jesus saith unto
her, Go, call thy husband, and come hither.[17] The woman answered and said, I have no husband. Jesus said unto her,
Thou hast well said, I have no husband:[18] For thou hast had five husbands; and he whom thou now hast is not thy
husband: in that saidst thou truly.[19] The woman saith unto him, Sir, I perceive that thou art a prophet.[20] Our fathers
worshipped in this mountain; and ye say, that in Jerusalem is the place where men ought to worship.[21] Jesus saith unto
her, Woman, believe me, the hour cometh, when ye shall neither in this mountain, nor yet at Jerusalem, worship the
Father.[22] Ye worship ye know not what: we know what we worship: for salvation is of the Jews.[23] But the hour cometh,
and now is, when the true worshippers shall worship the Father in spirit and in truth: for the Father seeketh such to
worship him.[24] God is a Spirit: and they that worship him must worship him in spirit and in truth.[25] The woman saith
unto him, I know that Messias cometh, which is called Christ: when he is come, he will tell us all things.[26] Jesus saith
unto her, I that speak unto thee am he.[27] And upon this came his disciples, and marvelled that he talked with the
woman: yet no man said, What seekest thou? or, Why talkest thou with her?[28] The woman then left her waterpot, and
went her way into the city, and saith to the men,[29] Come, see a man, which told me all things that ever I did: is not this
the Christ?

1 Corinthians 6:[19] What? know ye not that your body is the temple of the Holy Ghost which is in you, which ye have of God, and ye are not your own?

When or where does this story take place?

List the characters:

Important Words

Is there a problem?

What was the plot or main idea?

Why is this story important?

How can knowing this help me?

1 Corinthians 6:19 What? know ye not that your body is the temple of the Holy Ghost which is in you, which ye have of God, and ye are not your own?

Name:____________________

TEN TIMES BETTER

Write the letter of the correct match next to each problem.

1. ________	Jesus	a. The Son of God
2. ________	Lamb	b. A sacrifice for forgiveness
3. ________	Salvation	c. The act of being brought back to God
4. ________	Sin	d. Made free from sin
5. ________	Blood	e. The life source in a person
6. ________	Atonement	f. The act of making amends
7. ________	Reconciliation	g. Unmerited favor from God
8. ________	Grace	h. Divine and perfect
9. ________	Holy	i. The act of being saved from sin
10. ________	Redeemed	j. A wrong action against God's law

#5 JESUS SAYS, "FOLLOW ME".

MATTHEW 4:16 The people which sat in darkness saw great light; and to them which sat in the
region and shadow of death light is sprung up. 17 From that time Jesus began to preach, and to
say, Repent: for the kingdom of heaven is at hand. 18 And Jesus, walking by the sea of Galilee, saw
two brethren, Simon called Peter, and Andrew his brother, casting a net into the sea: for they
were fishers. 19 And he saith unto them, Follow me, and I will make you fishers of men. 20 And
they straightway left their nets, and followed him.

Jesus says, "Follow me."

Matthew 4:18-22; Mark 1:16-20; Luke 5:1-11; John 1:40-42

1 Corinthians 6:[19] What? know ye not that your body is the temple of the Holy Ghost which is in you, which ye have of God, and ye are not your own?

When or where does this story take place?

List the characters:

Important Words

Is there a problem?

What was the plot or main idea?

Why is this story important?

How can knowing this help me?

1 Corinthians 6:[19] What? know ye not that your body is the temple of the Holy Ghost which is in you, which ye have of God, and ye are not your own?

#6 DANIEL AND THE FIRERY FURNACE

Daniel 3:1 Nebuchadnezzar the king made an image of gold, whose height was threescore cubits, and the breadth thereof six cubits: he set it up in the plain of Dura, in the province of Babylon.[2] Then Nebuchadnezzar the king sent to gather together the princes, the governors, and the captains, the judges, the treasurers, the counsellors, the sheriffs, and all the rulers of the provinces, to come to the dedication of the image which Nebuchadnezzar the king had set up.[3] Then the princes, the governors, and captains, the judges, the treasurers, the counsellors, the sheriffs, and all the rulers of the provinces, were gathered together unto the dedication of the image that Nebuchadnezzar the king had set up; and they stood before the image that Nebuchadnezzar had set up.[4] Then an herald cried aloud, To you it is commanded, O people, nations, and languages,[5] That at what time ye hear the sound of the cornet, flute, harp, sackbut, psaltery, dulcimer, and all kinds of musick, ye fall down and worship the golden image that Nebuchadnezzar the king hath set up:[6] And whoso falleth not down and worshippeth shall the same hour be cast into the midst of a burning fiery furnace.[7] Therefore at that time, when all the people heard the sound of the cornet, flute, harp, sackbut, psaltery, and all kinds of musick, all the people, the nations, and the languages, fell down and worshipped the golden image that Nebuchadnezzar the king had set up.[8] Wherefore at that time certain Chaldeans came near, and accused the Jews.[9] They spake and said to the king Nebuchadnezzar, O king, live for ever.[10] Thou, O king, hast made a decree, that every man that shall hear the sound of the cornet, flute, harp, sackbut, psaltery, and dulcimer, and all kinds of musick, shall fall down and worship the golden image:[11] And whoso falleth not down and worshippeth, that he should be cast into the midst of a burning fiery furnace.[12] There are certain Jews whom thou hast set over the affairs of the province of Babylon, Shadrach, Meshach, and Abednego; these men, O king, have not regarded thee: they serve not thy gods, nor worship the golden image which thou hast set up.[13] Then Nebuchadnezzar in his rage and fury commanded to bring Shadrach, Meshach, and Abednego. Then they brought these men before the king.[14] Nebuchadnezzar spake and said unto them, Is it true, O Shadrach, Meshach, and Abednego, do not ye serve my gods, nor worship the golden image which I have set up?[15] Now if ye be ready that at what time ye hear the sound of the cornet, flute, harp, sackbut, psaltery, and dulcimer, and all kinds of musick, ye fall down and worship the image which I have made; well: but if ye worship not, ye shall be cast the same hour into the midst of a burning fiery furnace; and who is that God that shall deliver you out of my hands?[16] Shadrach, Meshach, and Abednego, answered and said to the king, O Nebuchadnezzar, we are not careful to answer thee in this matter.[17] If it be so, our God whom we serve is able to deliver us from the burning fiery furnace, and he will deliver us out of thine hand, O king.[18] But if not, be it known unto thee, O king, that we will not serve thy gods, nor worship the golden image which thou hast set up.[19] Then was Nebuchadnezzar full of fury, and the form of his visage was changed against Shadrach, Meshach, and Abednego: therefore he spake, and commanded that they should heat the furnace one seven times more than it was wont to be heated.[20] And he commanded the most mighty men that were in his army to bind Shadrach, Meshach, and Abednego, and to cast them into the burning fiery furnace.[21] Then these men were bound in their coats, their hosen, and their hats, and their other garments, and were cast into the midst of the burning fiery furnace.[22] Therefore because the king's commandment was urgent, and the furnace exceeding hot, the flames of the fire slew those men that took up Shadrach, Meshach, and Abednego.[23] And these three men, Shadrach, Meshach, and Abednego, fell down bound into the midst of the burning fiery furnace.[24] Then Nebuchadnezzar the king was astonished, and rose up in haste, and spake, and said unto his counsellors, Did not we cast three men bound into the midst of the fire? They answered and said unto the king, True, O king.[25] He answered and said, Lo, I see four men loose, walking in the midst of the fire, and they have no hurt; and the form of the fourth is like the Son of God.

[26] Then Nebuchadnezzar came near to the mouth of the burning fiery furnace, and spake, and said, Shadrach, Meshach, and Abednego, ye servants of the most high God, come forth, and come hither. Then Shadrach, Meshach, and Abednego, came forth of the midst of the fire.[27] And the princes, governors, and captains, and the king's counsellors, being gathered together, saw these men, upon whose bodies the fire had no power, nor was an hair of their head singed, neither were their coats changed, nor the smell of fire had passed on them.[28] Then Nebuchadnezzar spake, and said, Blessed be the God of Shadrach, Meshach, and Abednego, who hath sent his angel, and delivered his servants that trusted in him, and have changed the king's word, and yielded their bodies, that they might not serve nor worship any god, except their own God.[29] Therefore I make a decree, That every

people, nation, and language, which speak any thing amiss against the God of Shadrach, Meshach, and Abednego,
shall be cut in pieces, and their houses shall be made a dunghill: because there is no other God that can deliver after
this sort.30 Then the king promoted Shadrach, Meshach, and Abednego, in the province of Babylon.

When or where does this story take place?

List the characters:

1 Corinthians 6:[19] **What? know ye not that your body is the temple of the Holy Ghost which is in you, which ye have of God, and ye are not your own?**

Important Words

Is there a problem?

What was the plot or main idea?

Why is this story important?

How can knowing this help me?

1 Corinthians 6:[19] What? know ye not that your body is the temple of the Holy Ghost which is in you, which ye have of God, and ye are not your own?

#7 JOHN BAPTIZES JESUS

Matthew 3:[13] Then cometh Jesus from Galilee to Jordan unto John, to be baptized of him.[14] But
John forbad him, saying, I have need to be baptized of thee, and comest thou to me?[15] And Jesus
answering said unto him, Suffer it to be so now: for thus it becometh us to fulfil all righteousness.
Then he suffered him.[16] And Jesus, when he was baptized, went up straightway out of the water:
and, lo, the heavens were opened unto him, and he saw the Spirit of God descending like a dove,
and lighting upon him:[17] And lo a voice from heaven, saying, This is my beloved Son, in whom I am
well pleased.

1 Corinthians 6:[19] What? know ye not that your body is the temple of the Holy Ghost which is in you, which ye have of God, and ye are not your own?

When or where does this story take place?

List the characters:

Important Words

Is there a problem?

What was the plot or main idea?

Why is this story important?

How can knowing this help me?

#8 JOHN THE BAPTIST BIRTH ANNOUNCEMENT

Luke 1:5 There was in the days of Herod, the king of Judaea, a certain priest named Zacharias, of the course of Abia:
and his wife was of the daughters of Aaron, and her name was Elisabeth. 6 And they were both righteous before God,
walking in all the commandments and ordinances of the Lord blameless. 7 And they had no child, because that
Elisabeth was barren, and they both were now well stricken in years. 8 And it came to pass, that while he executed the
priest's office before God in the order of his course, 9 According to the custom of the priest's office, his lot was to
burn incense when he went into the temple of the Lord. 10 And the whole multitude of the people were praying
without at the time of incense. 11 And there appeared unto him an angel of the Lord standing on the right side of the
altar of incense. 12 And when Zacharias saw him, he was troubled, and fear fell upon him. 13 But the angel said unto
him, Fear not, Zacharias: for thy prayer is heard; and thy wife Elisabeth shall bear thee a son, and thou shalt call his
name John. 14 And thou shalt have joy and gladness; and many shall rejoice at his birth. 15 For he shall be great in the
sight of the Lord, and shall drink neither wine nor strong drink; and he shall be filled with the Holy Ghost, even from
his mother's womb. 16 And many of the children of Israel shall he turn to the Lord their God. 17 And he shall go before
him in the spirit and power of Elias, to turn the hearts of the fathers to the children, and the disobedient to the
wisdom of the just; to make ready a people prepared for the Lord. 18 And Zacharias said unto the angel, Whereby
shall I know this? for I am an old man, and my wife well stricken in years. 19 And the angel answering said unto him, I
am Gabriel, that stand in the presence of God; and am sent to speak unto thee, and to shew thee these glad
tidings. 20 And, behold, thou shalt be dumb, and not able to speak, until the day that these things shall be performed,
because thou believest not my words, which shall be fulfilled in their season. 21 And the people waited for Zacharias,
and marvelled that he tarried so long in the temple. 22 And when he came out, he could not speak unto them: and
they perceived that he had seen a vision in the temple: for he beckoned unto them, and remained speechless. 23 And
it came to pass, that, as soon as the days of his ministration were accomplished, he departed to his own
house. 24 And after those days his wife Elisabeth conceived, and hid herself five months, saying, 25 Thus hath the Lord
dealt with me in the days wherein he looked on me, to take away my reproach among men. 26 And in the sixth month
the angel Gabriel was sent from God unto a city of Galilee, named Nazareth, 27 To a virgin espoused to a man whose
name was Joseph, of the house of David; and the virgin's name was Mary. 28 And the angel came in unto her, and
said, Hail, thou that art highly favoured, the Lord is with thee: blessed art thou among women. 29 And when she saw
him, she was troubled at his saying, and cast in her mind what manner of salutation this should be. 30 And the angel
said unto her, Fear not, Mary: for thou hast found favour with God. 31 And, behold, thou shalt conceive in thy womb,
and bring forth a son, and shalt call his name JESUS. 32 He shall be great, and shall be called the Son of the Highest:
and the Lord God shall give unto him the throne of his father David: 33 And he shall reign over the house of Jacob for
ever; and of his kingdom there shall be no end.

1 Corinthians 6:[19] What? know ye not that your body is the temple of the Holy Ghost which is in you, which ye have of God, and ye are not your own?

[34] Then said Mary unto the angel, How shall this be, seeing I know not a man?[35] And the angel answered and said unto her, The Holy Ghost shall come upon thee, and the power of the Highest shall overshadow thee: therefore also that holy thing which shall be born of thee shall be called the Son of God.[36] And, behold, thy cousin Elisabeth, she hath also conceived a son in her old age: and this is the sixth month with her, who was called barren.[37] For with God nothing shall be impossible.

1 Corinthians 6:[19] What? know ye not that your body is the temple of the Holy Ghost which is in you, which ye have of God, and ye are not your own?

When or where does this story take place?

List the characters:

Important Words

Is there a problem?

What was the plot or main idea?

Why is this story important?

How can knowing this help me?

1 Corinthians 6:[19] What? know ye not that your body is the temple of the Holy Ghost which is in you, which ye have of God, and ye are not your own?

#9 MARY AND JOSEPH LOOK FOR JESUS

Luke 2:[41] Now his parents went to Jerusalem every year at the feast of the passover.[42] And when he was twelve years
old, they went up to Jerusalem after the custom of the feast.[43] And when they had fulfilled the days, as they returned,
the child Jesus tarried behind in Jerusalem; and Joseph and his mother knew not of it.[44] But they, supposing him to
have been in the company, went a day's journey; and they sought him among their kinsfolk and acquaintance.[45] And
when they found him not, they turned back again to Jerusalem, seeking him.[46] And it came to pass, that after three
days they found him in the temple, sitting in the midst of the doctors, both hearing them, and asking them
questions.[47] And all that heard him were astonished at his understanding and answers.[48] And when they saw him, they
were amazed: and his mother said unto him, Son, why hast thou thus dealt with us? behold, thy father and I have
sought thee sorrowing.[49] And he said unto them, How is it that ye sought me? wist ye not that I must be about my
Father's business?[50] And they understood not the saying which he spake unto them.[51] And he went down with them,
and came to Nazareth, and was subject unto them: but his mother kept all these sayings in her heart.[52] And Jesus
increased in wisdom and stature, and in favour with God and man.

1 Corinthians 6:[19] What? know ye not that your body is the temple of the Holy Ghost which is in you, which ye have of God, and ye are not your own?

When or where does this story take place?

List the characters:

Important Words

Is there a problem?

What was the plot or main idea?

Why is this story important?

How can knowing this help me?

1 Corinthians 6:[19] What? know ye not that your body is the temple of the Holy Ghost which is in you, which ye have of God, and ye are not your own?

#10 NEHEMIAH REBUILDS THE WALLS

Nehemiah 4:1 But it came to pass, that when Sanballat heard that we builded the wall, he was wroth, and took great
indignation, and mocked the Jews.[2] And he spake before his brethren and the army of Samaria, and said, What do
these feeble Jews? will they fortify themselves? will they sacrifice? will they make an end in a day? will they revive the
stones out of the heaps of the rubbish which are burned?[3] Now Tobiah the Ammonite was by him, and he said, Even
that which they build, if a fox go up, he shall even break down their stone wall.[4] Hear, O our God; for we are despised:
and turn their reproach upon their own head, and give them for a prey in the land of captivity:[5] And cover not their
iniquity, and let not their sin be blotted out from before thee: for they have provoked thee to anger before the
builders.[6] So built we the wall; and all the wall was joined together unto the half thereof: for the people had a mind to
work.[7] But it came to pass, that when Sanballat, and Tobiah, and the Arabians, and the Ammonites, and the Ashdodites,
heard that the walls of Jerusalem were made up, and that the breaches began to be stopped, then they were very
wroth,[8] And conspired all of them together to come and to fight against Jerusalem, and to hinder it.[9] Nevertheless we
made our prayer unto our God, and set a watch against them day and night, because of them.[10] And Judah said, The
strength of the bearers of burdens is decayed, and there is much rubbish; so that we are not able to build the
wall.[11] And our adversaries said, They shall not know, neither see, till we come in the midst among them, and slay them,
and cause the work to cease.[12] And it came to pass, that when the Jews which dwelt by them came, they said unto us
ten times, From all places whence ye shall return unto us they will be upon you.[13] Therefore set I in the lower places
behind the wall, and on the higher places, I even set the people after their families with their swords, their spears, and
their bows.[14] And I looked, and rose up, and said unto the nobles, and to the rulers, and to the rest of the people, Be
not ye afraid of them: remember the LORD, which is great and terrible, and fight for your brethren, your sons, and your
daughters, your wives, and your houses.[15] And it came to pass, when our enemies heard that it was known unto us, and
God had brought their counsel to nought, that we returned all of us to the wall, every one unto his work.[16] And it came
to pass from that time forth, that the half of my servants wrought in the work, and the other half of them held both the
spears, the shields, and the bows, and the habergeons; and the rulers were behind all the house of Judah.[17] They which
builded on the wall, and they that bare burdens, with those that laded, every one with one of his hands wrought in the
work, and with the other hand held a weapon.[18] For the builders, every one had his sword girded by his side, and so
builded. And he that sounded the trumpet was by me.[19] And I said unto the nobles, and to the rulers, and to the rest of
the people, The work is great and large, and we are separated upon the wall, one far from another.[20] In what place
therefore ye hear the sound of the trumpet, resort ye thither unto us: our God shall fight for us.[21] So we laboured in the
work: and half of them held the spears from the rising of the morning till the stars appeared.[22] Likewise at the same
time said I unto the people, Let every one with his servant lodge within Jerusalem, that in the night they may be a
guard to us, and labour on the day.[23] So neither I, nor my brethren, nor my servants, nor the men of the guard which
followed me, none of us put off our clothes, saving that every one put them off for washing.

1 Corinthians 6:[19] What? know ye not that your body is the temple of the Holy Ghost which is in you, which ye have of God, and ye are not your own?

Nehemiah rebuilds the walls.

Nehemiah 2:11—4:23

1 Corinthians 6:[19] What? know ye not that your body is the temple of the Holy Ghost which is in you, which ye have of God, and ye are not your own?

When or where does this story take place?

List the characters:

Important Words

Is there a problem?

What was the plot or main idea?

Why is this story important?

How can knowing this help me?

#11 JESUS IN THE WILDERNESS TEMPTATION

Matthew 4:1 Then was Jesus led up of the Spirit into the wilderness to be tempted of the devil.[2] And when he had
fasted forty days and forty nights, he was afterward an hungred.[3] And when the tempter came to him, he said, If thou
be the Son of God, command that these stones be made bread.[4] But he answered and said, It is written, Man shall not
live by bread alone, but by every word that proceedeth out of the mouth of God.[5] Then the devil taketh him up into the
holy city, and setteth him on a pinnacle of the temple,[6] And saith unto him, If thou be the Son of God, cast thyself
down: for it is written, He shall give his angels charge concerning thee: and in their hands they shall bear thee up, lest
at any time thou dash thy foot against a stone.[7] Jesus said unto him, It is written again, Thou shalt not tempt the Lord
thy God.[8] Again, the devil taketh him up into an exceeding high mountain, and sheweth him all the kingdoms of the
world, and the glory of them;[9] And saith unto him, All these things will I give thee, if thou wilt fall down and worship
me.[10] Then saith Jesus unto him, Get thee hence, Satan: for it is written, Thou shalt worship the Lord thy God, and him
only shalt thou serve.[11] Then the devil leaveth him, and, behold, angels came and ministered unto him.

1 Corinthians 6:[19] What? know ye not that your body is the temple of the Holy Ghost which is in you, which ye have of God, and ye are not your own?

When or where does this story take place?

List the characters:

Important Words

Is there a problem?

What was the plot or main idea?

Why is this story important?

How can knowing this help me?

1 Corinthians 6:[19] What? know ye not that your body is the temple of the Holy Ghost which is in you, which ye have of God, and ye are not your own?

#12 SAUL ON THE ROAD TO DAMASCUS

Acts 9:1 And Saul, yet breathing out threatenings and slaughter against the disciples of the Lord, went unto the high
priest,[2] And desired of him letters to Damascus to the synagogues, that if he found any of this way, whether they were
men or women, he might bring them bound unto Jerusalem.[3] And as he journeyed, he came near Damascus: and
suddenly there shined round about him a light from heaven:[4] And he fell to the earth, and heard a voice saying unto
him, Saul, Saul, why persecutest thou me?[5] And he said, Who art thou, Lord? And the Lord said, I am Jesus whom thou
persecutest: it is hard for thee to kick against the pricks.[6] And he trembling and astonished said, Lord, what wilt thou
have me to do? And the Lord said unto him, Arise, and go into the city, and it shall be told thee what thou must
do.[7] And the men which journeyed with him stood speechless, hearing a voice, but seeing no man.[8] And Saul arose
from the earth; and when his eyes were opened, he saw no man: but they led him by the hand, and brought him into
Damascus.[9] And he was three days without sight, and neither did eat nor drink.

1 Corinthians 6:[19] What? know ye not that your body is the temple of the Holy Ghost which is in you, which ye have of God, and ye are not your own?

When or where does this story take place?

List the characters:

Important Words

Is there a problem?

What was the plot or main idea?

Why is this story important?

How can knowing this help me?

1 Corinthians 6:19 What? know ye not that your body is the temple of the Holy Ghost which is in you, which ye have of God, and ye are not your own?

#13 LEAVE ALL

MARK 10: 23 And Jesus looked round about, and saith unto his disciples, How hardly shall
they that have riches enter into the kingdom of God! 24 And the disciples were astonished at his
words. But Jesus answereth again, and saith unto them, Children, how hard is it for them that trust
in riches to enter into the kingdom of God! 25 It is easier for a camel to go through the eye of a
needle, than for a rich man to enter into the kingdom of God. 26 And they were astonished out of
measure, saying among themselves, Who then can be saved? 27 And Jesus looking upon them saith,
With men it is impossible, but not with God: for with God all things are possible. 28 Then Peter
began to say unto him, Lo, we have left all, and have followed thee. 29 And Jesus answered and said,
Verily I say unto you, There is no man that hath left house, or brethren, or sisters, or father, or
mother, or wife, or children, or lands, for my sake, and the gospel's, 30 But he shall receive an
hundredfold now in this time, houses, and brethren, and sisters, and mothers, and children, and
lands, with persecutions; and in the world to come eternal life. 31 But many that are first shall be last;
and the last first.

DO NOT FELLOWSHIP WITH PEOPLE WHO DO NOT BELIEVE IN YOUR GOD.
YOU CAN WITNESS TO THEM!

1 Corinthians 6:19 What? know ye not that your body is the temple of the Holy Ghost which is in you, which ye have of God, and ye are not your own?

When or where does this story take place?

List the characters:

Important Words

Is there a problem?

What was the plot or main idea?

Why is this story important?

How can knowing this help me?

1 Corinthians 6:19 What? know ye not that your body is the temple of the Holy Ghost which is in you, which ye have of God, and ye are not your own?

#14 THE COMING DELIVERER

Genesis 3:1 Now the serpent was more subtil than any beast of the field which the LORD God
had made. And he said unto the woman, Yea, hath God said, Ye shall not eat of every tree of the
garden? 2 And the woman said unto the serpent, We may eat of the fruit of the trees of the
garden: 3 But of the fruit of the tree which is in the midst of the garden, God hath said, Ye shall
not eat of it, neither shall ye touch it, lest ye die. 4 And the serpent said unto the woman, Ye shall
not surely die: 5 For God doth know that in the day ye eat thereof, then your eyes shall be
opened, and ye shall be as gods, knowing good and evil. 6 And when the woman saw that the tree
was good for food, and that it was pleasant to the eyes, and a tree to be desired to make one
wise, she took of the fruit thereof, and did eat, and gave also unto her husband with her; and he
did eat. 7 And the eyes of them both were opened, and they knew that they were naked; and they
sewed fig leaves together, and made themselves aprons. 8 And they heard the voice of
the LORD God walking in the garden in the cool of the day: and Adam and his wife hid
themselves from the presence of the LORD God amongst the trees of the garden. 9 And
the LORD God called unto Adam, and said unto him, Where art thou? 10 And he said, I heard thy
voice in the garden, and I was afraid, because I was naked; and I hid myself. 11 And he said, Who
told thee that thou wast naked? Hast thou eaten of the tree, whereof I commanded thee that
thou shouldest not eat? 12 And the man said, The woman whom thou gavest to be with me, she
gave me of the tree, and I did eat. 13 And the LORD God said unto the woman, What is this that
thou hast done? And the woman said, The serpent beguiled me, and I did eat. 14 And
the LORD God said unto the serpent, Because thou hast done this, thou art cursed above all
cattle, and above every beast of the field; upon thy belly shalt thou go, and dust shalt thou eat all
the days of thy life: 15 And I will put enmity between thee and the woman, and between thy seed
and her seed; it shall bruise thy head, and thou shalt bruise his heel.

1 Corinthians 6:[19] What? know ye not that your body is the temple of the Holy Ghost which is in you, which ye have of God, and ye are not your own?

1 Corinthians 6:[19] What? know ye not that your body is the temple of the Holy Ghost which is in you, which ye have of God, and ye are not your own?

When or where does this story take place?

List the characters:

Important Words

Is there a problem?

What was the plot or main idea?

Why is this story important?

How can knowing this help me?

#15 THE SAVIOR WILL COME

Isaiah 9:[6] For unto us a child is born, unto us a son is given: and the government shall be upon his shoulder: and his name shall be called Wonderful, Counsellor, The mighty God, The everlasting Father, The Prince of Peace. [7] Of the increase of his government and peace there shall be no end, upon the throne of David, and upon his kingdom, to order it, and to establish it with judgment and with justice from henceforth even for ever. The zeal of the LORD of hosts will perform this.

1 Corinthians 6:[19] What? know ye not that your body is the temple of the Holy Ghost which is in you, which ye have of God, and ye are not your own?

When or where does this story take place?

List the characters:

Important Words

Is there a problem?

What was the plot or main idea?

Why is this story important?

How can knowing this help me?

#16 SAY NOT THAT YOU ARE A CHILD

Jeremiah 1:1 The words of Jeremiah the son of Hilkiah, of the priests that were in Anathoth in the
land of Benjamin:[2] To whom the word of the LORD came in the days of Josiah the son of Amon king
of Judah, in the thirteenth year of his reign.[3] It came also in the days of Jehoiakim the son of Josiah
king of Judah, unto the end of the eleventh year of Zedekiah the son of Josiah king of Judah, unto
the carrying away of Jerusalem captive in the fifth month.[4] Then the word of the LORD came unto
me, saying,[5] Before I formed thee in the belly I knew thee; and before thou camest forth out of the
womb I sanctified thee, and I ordained thee a prophet unto the nations.[6] Then said I, Ah, Lord GOD!
behold, I cannot speak: for I am a child.[7] But the LORD said unto me, Say not, I am a child: for thou
shalt go to all that I shall send thee, and whatsoever I command thee thou shalt speak.[8] Be not
afraid of their faces: for I am with thee to deliver thee, saith the LORD.[9] Then the LORD put forth his
hand, and touched my mouth. And the LORD said unto me, Behold, I have put my words in thy
mouth.[10] See, I have this day set thee over the nations and over the kingdoms, to root out, and to
pull down, and to destroy, and to throw down, to build, and to plant.

1 Corinthians 6:[19] What? know ye not that your body is the temple of the Holy Ghost which is in you, which ye have of God, and ye are not your own?

When or where does this story take place?

List the characters:

Important Words

Is there a problem?

What was the plot or main idea?

Why is this story important?

How can knowing this help me?

#17 YOU MAY ALWAYS BRING A SACRIFICE

Leviticus 6:[12] And the fire upon the altar shall be burning in it; it shall not be put out: and the priest shall burn wood on it every morning, and lay the burnt offering in order upon it; and he shall burn thereon the fat of the peace offerings.[13] The fire shall ever be burning upon the altar; it shall never go out.

#18 ISSAC IS OFFERED AND MAKES ABRAHAM THE FATHER OF FAITH.

Genesis 22:1 And it came to pass after these things, that God did tempt Abraham, and said unto
him, Abraham: and he said, Behold, here I am. 2 And he said, Take now thy son, thine only son Isaac,
whom thou lovest, and get thee into the land of Moriah; and offer him there for a burnt offering
upon one of the mountains which I will tell thee of. 3 And Abraham rose up early in the morning,
and saddled his ass, and took two of his young men with him, and Isaac his son, and clave the
wood for the burnt offering, and rose up, and went unto the place of which God had told
him. 4 Then on the third day Abraham lifted up his eyes, and saw the place afar off. 5 And Abraham
said unto his young men, Abide ye here with the ass; and I and the lad will go yonder and worship,
and come again to you. 6 And Abraham took the wood of the burnt offering, and laid it upon Isaac
his son; and he took the fire in his hand, and a knife; and they went both of them together. 7 And
Isaac spake unto Abraham his father, and said, My father: and he said, Here am I, my son. And he
said, Behold the fire and the wood: but where is the lamb for a burnt offering? 8 And Abraham said,
My son, God will provide himself a lamb for a burnt offering: so they went both of them
together. 9 And they came to the place which God had told him of; and Abraham built an altar there,
and laid the wood in order, and bound Isaac his son, and laid him on the altar upon the
wood. 10 And Abraham stretched forth his hand, and took the knife to slay his son. 11 And the angel
of the LORD called unto him out of heaven, and said, Abraham, Abraham: and he said, Here am
I. 12 And he said, Lay not thine hand upon the lad, neither do thou any thing unto him: for now I
know that thou fearest God, seeing thou hast not withheld thy son, thine only son from me. 13 And
Abraham lifted up his eyes, and looked, and behold behind him a ram caught in a thicket by his
horns: and Abraham went and took the ram, and offered him up for a burnt offering in the stead of
his son.

1 Corinthians 6:[19] **What? know ye not that your body is the temple of the Holy Ghost which is in you, which ye have of God, and ye are not your own?**

Abram offered sacrifices to the Lord for being chosen as "The Father of His People"

1 Corinthians 6:[19] **What? know ye not that your body is the temple of the Holy Ghost which is in you, which ye have of God, and ye are not your own?**

When or where does this story take place?

List the characters:

Important Words

Is there a problem?

What was the plot or main idea?

Why is this story important?

How can knowing this help me?

#19 LET MY PEOPLE GO!

Exodus 9:1 Then the LORD said unto Moses, Go in unto Pharaoh, and tell him, Thus saith
the LORD God of the Hebrews, Let my people go, that they may serve me.[2] For if thou refuse to let
them go, and wilt hold them still,[3] Behold, the hand of the LORD is upon thy cattle which is in the
field, upon the horses, upon the asses, upon the camels, upon the oxen, and upon the sheep: there
shall be a very grievous murrain.[4] And the LORD shall sever between the cattle of Israel and the
cattle of Egypt: and there shall nothing die of all that is the children's of Israel.[5] And
the LORD appointed a set time, saying, To morrow the LORD shall do this thing in the land.[6] And
the LORD did that thing on the morrow, and all the cattle of Egypt died: but of the cattle of the
children of Israel died not one.[7] And Pharaoh sent, and, behold, there was not one of the cattle of
the Israelites dead. And the heart of Pharaoh was hardened, and he did not let the people go.

1 Corinthians 6:19 What? know ye not that your body is the temple of the Holy Ghost which is in you, which ye have of God, and ye are not your own?

When or where does this story take place?

List the characters:

Important Words

Is there a problem?

What was the plot or main idea?

Why is this story important?

How can knowing this help me?

1 Corinthians 6:[19] What? know ye not that your body is the temple of the Holy Ghost which is in you, which ye have of God, and ye are not your own?

#20 THE LORD COMMANDS THE PEOPLE

Exodus 20:1 And God spake all these words, saying,[2] I am the LORD thy God, which have brought thee out of
the land of Egypt, out of the house of bondage.[3] Thou shalt have no other gods before me.[4] Thou shalt not
make unto thee any graven image, or any likeness of any thing that is in heaven above, or that is in the
earth beneath, or that is in the water under the earth.[5] Thou shalt not bow down thyself to them, nor serve
them: for I the LORD thy God am a jealous God, visiting the iniquity of the fathers upon the children unto the
third and fourth generation of them that hate me;[6] And shewing mercy unto thousands of them that love
me, and keep my commandments.[7] Thou shalt not take the name of the LORD thy God in vain; for
the LORD will not hold him guiltless that taketh his name in vain.[8] Remember the sabbath day, to keep it
holy.[9] Six days shalt thou labour, and do all thy work:[10] But the seventh day is the sabbath of the LORD thy
God: in it thou shalt not do any work, thou, nor thy son, nor thy daughter, thy manservant, nor thy
maidservant, nor thy cattle, nor thy stranger that is within thy gates:[11] For in six days the LORD made heaven
and earth, the sea, and all that in them is, and rested the seventh day: wherefore the LORD blessed the
sabbath day, and hallowed it.[12] Honour thy father and thy mother: that thy days may be long upon the land
which the LORD thy God giveth thee.[13] Thou shalt not kill.[14] Thou shalt not commit adultery.[15] Thou shalt not
steal.[16] Thou shalt not bear false witness against thy neighbour.[17] Thou shalt not covet thy neighbour's
house, thou shalt not covet thy neighbour's wife, nor his manservant, nor his maidservant, nor his ox, nor his
ass, nor any thing that is thy neighbour's.[18] And all the people saw the thunderings, and the lightnings, and
the noise of the trumpet, and the mountain smoking: and when the people saw it, they removed, and stood
afar off.[19] And they said unto Moses, Speak thou with us, and we will hear: but let not God speak with us, lest
we die.[20] And Moses said unto the people, Fear not: for God is come to prove you, and that his fear may be
before your faces, that ye sin not.[21] And the people stood afar off, and Moses drew near unto the thick
darkness where God was.[22] And the LORD said unto Moses, Thus thou shalt say unto the children of Israel, Ye
have seen that I have talked with you from heaven.[23] Ye shall not make with me gods of silver, neither shall
ye make unto you gods of gold.[24] An altar of earth thou shalt make unto me, and shalt sacrifice thereon thy
burnt offerings, and thy peace offerings, thy sheep, and thine oxen: in all places where I record my name I
will come unto thee, and I will bless thee.[25] And if thou wilt make me an altar of stone, thou shalt not build it
of hewn stone: for if thou lift up thy tool upon it, thou hast polluted it.[26] Neither shalt thou go up by steps
unto mine altar, that thy nakedness be not discovered thereon.

1 Corinthians 6:[19] What? know ye not that your body is the temple of the Holy Ghost which is in you, which ye have of God, and ye are not your own?

1 Corinthians 6:[19] What? know ye not that your body is the temple of the Holy Ghost which is in you, which ye have of God, and ye are not your own?

When or where does this story take place?

List the characters:

Important Words

Is there a problem?

What was the plot or main idea?

Why is this story important?

How can knowing this help me?

#21 THE PRODIGAL SON

Luke 15:11 And he said, A certain man had two sons:[12] And the younger of them said to his father,
Father, give me the portion of goods that falleth to me. And he divided unto them his living.[13] And
not many days after the younger son gathered all together, and took his journey into a far country,
and there wasted his substance with riotous living.[14] And when he had spent all, there arose a
mighty famine in that land; and he began to be in want.[15] And he went and joined himself to a
citizen of that country; and he sent him into his fields to feed swine.[16] And he would fain have filled
his belly with the husks that the swine did eat: and no man gave unto him.[17] And when he came to
himself, he said, How many hired servants of my father's have bread enough and to spare, and I
perish with hunger![18] I will arise and go to my father, and will say unto him, Father, I have sinned
against heaven, and before thee,[19] And am no more worthy to be called thy son: make me as one
of thy hired servants.[20] And he arose, and came to his father. But when he was yet a great way off,
his father saw him, and had compassion, and ran, and fell on his neck, and kissed him.[21] And the
son said unto him, Father, I have sinned against heaven, and in thy sight, and am no more worthy
to be called thy son.[22] But the father said to his servants, Bring forth the best robe, and put it on
him; and put a ring on his hand, and shoes on his feet:[23] And bring hither the fatted calf, and kill it;
and let us eat, and be merry:[24] For this my son was dead, and is alive again; he was lost, and is
found. And they began to be merry.[25] Now his elder son was in the field: and as he came and drew
nigh to the house, he heard musick and dancing.[26] And he called one of the servants, and asked
what these things meant.[27] And he said unto him, Thy brother is come; and thy father hath killed
the fatted calf, because he hath received him safe and sound.[28] And he was angry, and would not
go in: therefore came his father out, and intreated him.[29] And he answering said to his father, Lo,
these many years do I serve thee, neither transgressed I at any time thy commandment: and yet
thou never gavest me a kid, that I might make merry with my friends:[30] But as soon as this thy son
was come, which hath devoured thy living with harlots, thou hast killed for him the fatted
calf.[31] And he said unto him, Son, thou art ever with me, and all that I have is thine.[32] It was meet
that we should make merry, and be glad: for this thy brother was dead, and is alive again; and was
lost, and is found.

1 Corinthians 6:[19] What? know ye not that your body is the temple of the Holy Ghost which is in you, which ye have of God, and ye are not your own?

1 Corinthians 6:[19] What? know ye not that your body is the temple of the Holy Ghost which is in you, which ye have of God, and ye are not your own?

When or where does this story take place?

List the characters:

Important Words

Is there a problem?

What was the plot or main idea?

Why is this story important?

How can knowing this help me?

#22 WALLS OF JERICHO

Joshua 6:1 Now Jericho was straitly shut up because of the children of Israel: none went out, and none came in.[2] And the LORD said unto Joshua, See, I have given into thine hand Jericho, and the king thereof, and the mighty men of valour.[3] And ye shall compass the city, all ye men of war, and go round about the city once. Thus shalt thou do six days.[4] And seven priests shall bear before the ark seven trumpets of rams' horns: and the seventh day ye shall compass the city seven times, and the priests shall blow with the trumpets.[5] And it shall come to pass, that when they make a long blast with the ram's horn, and when ye hear the sound of the trumpet, all the people shall shout with a great shout; and the wall of the city shall fall down flat, and the people shall ascend up every man straight before him.

1 Corinthians 6:19 What? know ye not that your body is the temple of the Holy Ghost which is in you, which ye have of God, and ye are not your own?

When or where does this story take place?

List the characters:

Important Words

Is there a problem?

What was the plot or main idea?

Why is this story important?

How can knowing this help me?

#23 GIDEON THE JUDGE AND HE DID NOT EVEN KNOW IT!

Judges 6:1 And the children of Israel did evil in the sight of the LORD: and the LORD delivered them
into the hand of Midian seven years.[2] And the hand of Midian prevailed against Israel: and because
of the Midianites the children of Israel made them the dens which are in the mountains, and caves,
and strong holds.[3] And so it was, when Israel had sown, that the Midianites came up, and the
Amalekites, and the children of the east, even they came up against them;[4] And they encamped
against them, and destroyed the increase of the earth, till thou come unto Gaza, and left no
sustenance for Israel, neither sheep, nor ox, nor ass.[5] For they came up with their cattle and their
tents, and they came as grasshoppers for multitude; for both they and their camels were without
number: and they entered into the land to destroy it.[6] And Israel was greatly impoverished because
of the Midianites; and the children of Israel cried unto the LORD.[7] And it came to pass, when the
children of Israel cried unto the LORD because of the Midianites,[8] That the LORD sent a prophet unto
the children of Israel, which said unto them, Thus saith the LORD God of Israel, I brought you up
from Egypt, and brought you forth out of the house of bondage;[9] And I delivered you out of the
hand of the Egyptians, and out of the hand of all that oppressed you, and drave them out from
before you, and gave you their land;[10] And I said unto you, I am the LORD your God; fear not the
gods of the Amorites, in whose land ye dwell: but ye have not obeyed my voice.[11] And there came
an angel of the LORD, and sat under an oak which was in Ophrah, that pertained unto Joash the
Abiezrite: and his son Gideon threshed wheat by the winepress, to hide it from the
Midianites.[12] And the angel of the LORD appeared unto him, and said unto him, The LORD is with
thee, thou mighty man of valour.[13] And Gideon said unto him, Oh my Lord, if the LORD be with us,
why then is all this befallen us? and where be all his miracles which our fathers told us of, saying,
Did not the LORD bring us up from Egypt? but now the LORD hath forsaken us, and delivered us into
the hands of the Midianites.[14] And the LORD looked upon him, and said, Go in this thy might, and
thou shalt save Israel from the hand of the Midianites: have not I sent thee?[15] And he said unto him,
Oh my Lord, wherewith shall I save Israel? behold, my family is poor in Manasseh, and I am the
least in my father's house.[16] And the LORD said unto him, Surely I will be with thee, and thou shalt
smite the Midianites as one man.[17] And he said unto him, If now I have found grace in thy sight,
then shew me a sign that thou talkest with me.[18] Depart not hence, I pray thee, until I come unto
thee, and bring forth my present, and set it before thee. And he said, I will tarry until thou come
again.[19] And Gideon went in, and made ready a kid, and unleavened cakes of an ephah of flour: the
flesh he put in a basket, and he put the broth in a pot, and brought it out unto him under the oak,
and presented it.[20] And the angel of God said unto him, Take the flesh and the unleavened cakes,
and lay them upon this rock, and pour out the broth. And he did so.[21] Then the angel of
the LORD put forth the end of the staff that was in his hand, and touched the flesh and the
unleavened cakes; and there rose up fire out of the rock, and consumed the flesh and the
unleavened cakes. Then the angel of the LORD departed out of his sight.[22] And when Gideon
perceived that he was an angel of the LORD, Gideon said, Alas, O LORD God! for because I have seen
an angel of the LORD face to face.[23] And the LORD said unto him, Peace be unto thee; fear not: thou

shalt not die.[24] Then Gideon built an altar there unto the LORD, and called it Jehovahshalom: unto this day it is yet in Ophrah of the Abiezrites.

God helped Gideon be courageous.

1 Corinthians 6:[19] What? know ye not that your body is the temple of the Holy Ghost which is in you, which ye have of God, and ye are not your own?

When or where does this story take place?

List the characters:

Important Words

Is there a problem?

What was the plot or main idea?

Why is this story important?

How can knowing this help me?

#24 RUTH THE DAUGHTER IN LAW OF NAOMI

Ruth 1:1 Now it came to pass in the days when the judges ruled, that there was a famine in the
land. And a certain man of Bethlehemjudah went to sojourn in the country of Moab, he, and his
wife, and his two sons.[2] And the name of the man was Elimelech, and the name of his wife Naomi,
and the name of his two sons Mahlon and Chilion, Ephrathites of Bethlehemjudah. And they came
into the country of Moab, and continued there.[3] And Elimelech Naomi's husband died; and she was
left, and her two sons.[4] And they took them wives of the women of Moab; the name of the one was
Orpah, and the name of the other Ruth: and they dwelled there about ten years.[5] And Mahlon and
Chilion died also both of them; and the woman was left of her two sons and her husband.[6] Then
she arose with her daughters in law, that she might return from the country of Moab: for she had
heard in the country of Moab how that the LORD had visited his people in giving them
bread.[7] Wherefore she went forth out of the place where she was, and her two daughters in law
with her; and they went on the way to return unto the land of Judah.[8] And Naomi said unto her two
daughters in law, Go, return each to her mother's house: the LORD deal kindly with you, as ye have
dealt with the dead, and with me.[9] The LORD grant you that ye may find rest, each of you in the
house of her husband. Then she kissed them; and they lifted up their voice, and wept.[10] And they
said unto her, Surely we will return with thee unto thy people.[11] And Naomi said, Turn again, my
daughters: why will ye go with me? are there yet any more sons in my womb, that they may be
your husbands?[12] Turn again, my daughters, go your way; for I am too old to have an husband. If I
should say, I have hope, if I should have an husband also to night, and should also bear
sons;[13] Would ye tarry for them till they were grown? would ye stay for them from having
husbands? nay, my daughters; for it grieveth me much for your sakes that the hand of the LORD is
gone out against me.[14] And they lifted up their voice, and wept again: and Orpah kissed her mother
in law; but Ruth clave unto her.[15] And she said, Behold, thy sister in law is gone back unto her
people, and unto her gods: return thou after thy sister in law.[16] And Ruth said, Intreat me not to
leave thee, or to return from following after thee: for whither thou goest, I will go; and where thou
lodgest, I will lodge: thy people shall be my people, and thy God my God:[17] Where thou diest, will I
die, and there will I be buried: the LORD do so to me, and more also, if ought but death part thee
and me.[18] When she saw that she was stedfastly minded to go with her, then she left speaking unto
her.

1 Corinthians 6:19 What? know ye not that your body is the temple of the Holy Ghost which is in you, which ye have of God, and ye are not your own?

Entreat me not to leave you, or to turn back from following after you; for whereever you go, I will go; and whereever you lodge, I will lodge; your people shall be my people, and your God will be my God.

Ruth 1:16

1 Corinthians 6:[19] What? know ye not that your body is the temple of the Holy Ghost which is in you, which ye have of God, and ye are not your own?

When or where does this story take place?

List the characters:

Important Words

Is there a problem?

What was the plot or main idea?

Why is this story important?

How can knowing this help me?

1 Corinthians 6:19 What? know ye not that your body is the temple of the Holy Ghost which is in you, which ye have of God, and ye are not your own?

#25 THE CHILD SAMUEL

4 That the LORD called Samuel: and he answered, Here am I. 5 And he ran unto Eli, and said, Here am
I; for thou calledst me. And he said, I called not; lie down again. And he went and lay down. 6 And
the LORD called yet again, Samuel. And Samuel arose and went to Eli, and said, Here am I; for thou
didst call me. And he answered, I called not, my son; lie down again. 7 Now Samuel did not yet know
the LORD, neither was the word of the LORD yet revealed unto him. 8 And the LORD called Samuel
again the third time. And he arose and went to Eli, and said, Here am I; for thou didst call me. And
Eli perceived that the LORD had called the child. 9 Therefore Eli said unto Samuel, Go, lie down: and it
shall be, if he call thee, that thou shalt say, Speak, LORD; for thy servant heareth. So Samuel went
and lay down in his place. 10 And the LORD came, and stood, and called as at other times, Samuel,
Samuel. Then Samuel answered, Speak; for thy servant heareth. 11 And the LORD said to Samuel,
Behold, I will do a thing in Israel, at which both the ears of every one that heareth it shall tingle.

1 Corinthians 6:[19] What? know ye not that your body is the temple of the Holy Ghost which is in you, which ye have of God, and ye are not your own?

When or where does this story take place?

List the characters:

Important Words

Is there a problem?

What was the plot or main idea?

Why is this story important?

How can knowing this help me?

26 EZRA THE LORDS PRIEST

Ezra 7:1 Now after these things, in the reign of Artaxerxes king of Persia, Ezra the son of Seraiah,
the son of Azariah, the son of Hilkiah,[2] The son of Shallum, the son of Zadok, the son of
Ahitub,[3] The son of Amariah, the son of Azariah, the son of Meraioth,[4] The son of Zerahiah, the son
of Uzzi, the son of Bukki,[5] The son of Abishua, the son of Phinehas, the son of Eleazar, the son of
Aaron the chief priest:[6] This Ezra went up from Babylon; and he was a ready scribe in the law of
Moses, which the LORD God of Israel had given: and the king granted him all his request, according
to the hand of the LORD his God upon him.[7] And there went up some of the children of Israel, and
of the priests, and the Levites, and the singers, and the porters, and the Nethinims, unto Jerusalem,
in the seventh year of Artaxerxes the king.[8] And he came to Jerusalem in the fifth month, which was
in the seventh year of the king.[9] For upon the first day of the first month began he to go up from
Babylon, and on the first day of the fifth month came he to Jerusalem, according to the good hand
of his God upon him.[10] For Ezra had prepared his heart to seek the law of the LORD, and to do it,
and to teach in Israel statutes and judgments.[11] Now this is the copy of the letter that the king
Artaxerxes gave unto Ezra the priest, the scribe, even a scribe of the words of the commandments
of the LORD, and of his statutes to Israel.[12] Artaxerxes, king of kings, unto Ezra the priest, a scribe of
the law of the God of heaven, perfect peace, and at such a time.[13] I make a decree, that all they of
the people of Israel, and of his priests and Levites, in my realm, which are minded of their own
freewill to go up to Jerusalem, go with thee.[14] Forasmuch as thou art sent of the king, and of his
seven counsellors, to enquire concerning Judah and Jerusalem, according to the law of thy God
which is in thine hand;[15] And to carry the silver and gold, which the king and his counsellors have
freely offered unto the God of Israel, whose habitation is in Jerusalem,[16] And all the silver and gold
that thou canst find in all the province of Babylon, with the freewill offering of the people, and of
the priests, offering willingly for the house of their God which is in Jerusalem:[17] That thou mayest
buy speedily with this money bullocks, rams, lambs, with their meat offerings and their drink
offerings, and offer them upon the altar of the house of your God which is in Jerusalem.[18] And
whatsoever shall seem good to thee, and to thy brethren, to do with the rest of the silver and the
gold, that do after the will of your God.[19] The vessels also that are given thee for the service of the
house of thy God, those deliver thou before the God of Jerusalem.[20] And whatsoever more shall be
needful for the house of thy God, which thou shalt have occasion to bestow, bestow it out of the
king's treasure house.[21] And I, even I Artaxerxes the king, do make a decree to all the treasurers
which are beyond the river, that whatsoever Ezra the priest, the scribe of the law of the God of
heaven, shall require of you, it be done speedily,

1 Corinthians 6:[19] What? know ye not that your body is the temple of the Holy Ghost which is in you, which ye have of God, and ye are not your own?

Ezra read the law.

1 Corinthians 6:[19] What? know ye not that your body is the temple of the Holy Ghost which is in you, which ye have of God, and ye are not your own?

When or where does this story take place?

List the characters:

Important Words

Is there a problem?

What was the plot or main idea?

Why is this story important?

How can knowing this help me?

#26 NEHEMIAH CRITICISED WHILE HE BUILDS THE WAll

Nehemiah 4:1 But it came to pass, that when Sanballat heard that we builded the wall, he was
wroth, and took great indignation, and mocked the Jews.[2] And he spake before his brethren and
the army of Samaria, and said, What do these feeble Jews? will they fortify themselves? will they
sacrifice? will they make an end in a day? will they revive the stones out of the heaps of the rubbish
which are burned?[3] Now Tobiah the Ammonite was by him, and he said, Even that which they build,
if a fox go up, he shall even break down their stone wall.[4] Hear, O our God; for we are despised: and
turn their reproach upon their own head, and give them for a prey in the land of captivity:[5] And
cover not their iniquity, and let not their sin be blotted out from before thee: for they have
provoked thee to anger before the builders.[6] So built we the wall; and all the wall was joined
together unto the half thereof: for the people had a mind to work.[7] But it came to pass, that when
Sanballat, and Tobiah, and the Arabians, and the Ammonites, and the Ashdodites, heard that the
walls of Jerusalem were made up, and that the breaches began to be stopped, then they were very
wroth,[8] And conspired all of them together to come and to fight against Jerusalem, and to hinder
it.[9] Nevertheless we made our prayer unto our God, and set a watch against them day and night,
because of them.[10] And Judah said, The strength of the bearers of burdens is decayed, and there is
much rubbish; so that we are not able to build the wall.[11] And our adversaries said, They shall not
know, neither see, till we come in the midst among them, and slay them, and cause the work to
cease.[12] And it came to pass, that when the Jews which dwelt by them came, they said unto us ten
times, From all places whence ye shall return unto us they will be upon you.[13] Therefore set I in the
lower places behind the wall, and on the higher places, I even set the people after their families
with their swords, their spears, and their bows.[14] And I looked, and rose up, and said unto the
nobles, and to the rulers, and to the rest of the people, Be not ye afraid of them: remember
the LORD, which is great and terrible, and fight for your brethren, your sons, and your daughters,
your wives, and your houses.[15] And it came to pass, when our enemies heard that it was known
unto us, and God had brought their counsel to nought, that we returned all of us to the wall, every
one unto his work.[16] And it came to pass from that time forth, that the half of my servants wrought
in the work, and the other half of them held both the spears, the shields, and the bows, and the
habergeons; and the rulers were behind all the house of Judah.[17] They which builded on the wall,
and they that bare burdens, with those that laded, every one with one of his hands wrought in the
work, and with the other hand held a weapon.[18] For the builders, every one had his sword girded by
his side, and so builded. And he that sounded the trumpet was by me.

1 Corinthians 6:[19] What? know ye not that your body is the temple of the Holy Ghost which is in you, which ye have of God, and ye are not your own?

1 Corinthians 6:[19] What? know ye not that your body is the temple of the Holy Ghost which is in you, which ye have of God, and ye are not your own?

When or where does this story take place?

List the characters:

Important Words

Is there a problem?

What was the plot or main idea?

Why is this story important?

How can knowing this help me?

#27 ESTER THE QUEEN

Esther 4:1 When Mordecai perceived all that was done, Mordecai rent his clothes, and put on
sackcloth with ashes, and went out into the midst of the city, and cried with a loud and a bitter
cry;[2] And came even before the king's gate: for none might enter into the king's gate clothed with
sackcloth.[3] And in every province, whithersoever the king's commandment and his decree came,
there was great mourning among the Jews, and fasting, and weeping, and wailing; and many lay in
sackcloth and ashes.[4] So Esther's maids and her chamberlains came and told it her. Then was the
queen exceedingly grieved; and she sent raiment to clothe Mordecai, and to take away his
sackcloth from him: but he received it not.[5] Then called Esther for Hatach, one of the king's
chamberlains, whom he had appointed to attend upon her, and gave him a commandment to
Mordecai, to know what it was, and why it was.[6] So Hatach went forth to Mordecai unto the street
of the city, which was before the king's gate.[7] And Mordecai told him of all that had happened unto
him, and of the sum of the money that Haman had promised to pay to the king's treasuries for the
Jews, to destroy them.[8] Also he gave him the copy of the writing of the decree that was given at
Shushan to destroy them, to shew it unto Esther, and to declare it unto her, and to charge her that
she should go in unto the king, to make supplication unto him, and to make request before him for
her people.[9] And Hatach came and told Esther the words of Mordecai.[10] Again Esther spake unto
Hatach, and gave him commandment unto Mordecai;[11] All the king's servants, and the people of
the king's provinces, do know, that whosoever, whether man or women, shall come unto the king
into the inner court, who is not called, there is one law of his to put him to death, except such to
whom the king shall hold out the golden sceptre, that he may live: but I have not been called to
come in unto the king these thirty days.[12] And they told to Mordecai Esther's words.[13] Then
Mordecai commanded to answer Esther, Think not with thyself that thou shalt escape in the king's
house, more than all the Jews.[14] For if thou altogether holdest thy peace at this time, then shall
there enlargement and deliverance arise to the Jews from another place; but thou and thy father's
house shall be destroyed: and who knoweth whether thou art come to the kingdom for such a time
as this?[15] Then Esther bade them return Mordecai this answer,[16] Go, gather together all the Jews
that are present in Shushan, and fast ye for me, and neither eat nor drink three days, night or day: I
also and my maidens will fast likewise; and so will I go in unto the king, which is not according to
the law: and if I perish, I perish.[17] So Mordecai went his way, and did according to all that Esther
had commanded him.

1 Corinthians 6:[19] What? know ye not that your body is the temple of the Holy Ghost which is in you, which ye have of God, and ye are not your own?

Queen Esther was willing to give her own life to save the lives of many others.

1 Corinthians 6:[19] What? know ye not that your body is the temple of the Holy Ghost which is in you, which ye have of God, and ye are not your own?

When or where does this story take place?

List the characters:

Important Words

Is there a problem?

What was the plot or main idea?

Why is this story important?

How can knowing this help me?

#28 ELIJAH AND JEZEBEL

1 Kings 19:1 And Ahab told Jezebel all that Elijah had done, and withal how he had slain all the
prophets with the sword. 2 Then Jezebel sent a messenger unto Elijah, saying, So let the gods do to me, and
more also, if I make not thy life as the life of one of them by to morrow about this time. 3 And when he saw
that, he arose, and went for his life, and came to Beersheba, which belongeth to Judah, and left his servant
there. 4 But he himself went a day's journey into the wilderness, and came and sat down under a juniper tree:
and he requested for himself that he might die; and said, It is enough; now, O LORD, take away my life; for I
am not better than my fathers. 5 And as he lay and slept under a juniper tree, behold, then an angel touched
him, and said unto him, Arise and eat. 6 And he looked, and, behold, there was a cake baken on the coals,
and a cruse of water at his head. And he did eat and drink, and laid him down again. 7 And the angel of
the LORD came again the second time, and touched him, and said, Arise and eat; because the journey is too
great for thee. 8 And he arose, and did eat and drink, and went in the strength of that meat forty days and
forty nights unto Horeb the mount of God. 9 And he came thither unto a cave, and lodged there; and,
behold, the word of the LORD came to him, and he said unto him, What doest thou here, Elijah? 10 And he
said, I have been very jealous for the LORD God of hosts: for the children of Israel have forsaken thy
covenant, thrown down thine altars, and slain thy prophets with the sword; and I, even I only, am left; and
they seek my life, to take it away. 11 And he said, Go forth, and stand upon the mount before the LORD. And,
behold, the LORD passed by, and a great and strong wind rent the mountains, and brake in pieces the rocks
before the LORD; but the LORD was not in the wind: and after the wind an earthquake; but the LORD was not
in the earthquake: 12 And after the earthquake a fire; but the LORD was not in the fire: and after the fire a still
small voice. 13 And it was so, when Elijah heard it, that he wrapped his face in his mantle, and went out, and
stood in the entering in of the cave. And, behold, there came a voice unto him, and said, What doest thou
here, Elijah? 14 And he said, I have been very jealous for the LORD God of hosts: because the children of Israel
have forsaken thy covenant, thrown down thine altars, and slain thy prophets with the sword; and I, even I
only, am left; and they seek my life, to take it away. 15 And the LORD said unto him, Go, return on thy way to
the wilderness of Damascus: and when thou comest, anoint Hazael to be king over Syria:

1 Corinthians 6:[19] What? know ye not that your body is the temple of the Holy Ghost which is in you, which ye have of God, and ye are not your own?

1 Corinthians 6:[19] What? know ye not that your body is the temple of the Holy Ghost which is in you, which ye have of God, and ye are not your own?

When or where does this story take place?

List the characters:

Important Words

Is there a problem?

What was the plot or main idea?

Why is this story important?

How can knowing this help me?

#28 FIRE ON THE MOUNTAIN

I KINGS 18:14 And now thou sayest, Go, tell thy lord, Behold, Elijah is here: and he shall slay me.[15] And Elijah said, As the LORD of hosts liveth, before whom I stand, I will surely shew myself unto him to day.[16] So Obadiah went to meet Ahab, and told him: and Ahab went to meet Elijah.[17] And it came to pass, when Ahab saw Elijah, that Ahab said unto him, Art thou he that troubleth Israel?[18] And he answered, I have not troubled Israel; but thou, and thy father's house, in that ye have forsaken the commandments of the LORD, and thou hast followed Baalim.[19] Now therefore send, and gather to me all Israel unto mount Carmel, and the prophets of Baal four hundred and fifty, and the prophets of the groves four hundred, which eat at Jezebel's table.[20] So Ahab sent unto all the children of Israel, and gathered the prophets together unto mount Carmel.[21] And Elijah came unto all the people, and said, How long halt ye between two opinions? if the LORD be God, follow him: but if Baal, then follow him. And the people answered him not a word.[22] Then said Elijah unto the people, I, even I only, remain a prophet of the LORD; but Baal's prophets are four hundred and fifty men.[23] Let them therefore give us two bullocks; and let them choose one bullock for themselves, and cut it in pieces, and lay it on wood, and put no fire under: and I will dress the other bullock, and lay it on wood, and put no fire under:[24] And call ye on the name of your gods, and I will call on the name of the LORD: and the God that answereth by fire, let him be God. And all the people answered and said, It is well spoken.[25] And Elijah said unto the prophets of Baal, Choose you one bullock for yourselves, and dress it first; for ye are many; and call on the name of your gods, but put no fire under.[26] And they took the bullock which was given them, and they dressed it, and called on the name of Baal from morning even until noon, saying, O Baal, hear us. But there was no voice, nor any that answered. And they leaped upon the altar which was made.[27] And it came to pass at noon, that Elijah mocked them, and said, Cry aloud: for he is a god; either he is talking, or he is pursuing, or he is in a journey, or peradventure he sleepeth, and must beawaked.[28] And they cried aloud, and cut themselves after their manner with knives and lancets, till the blood gushed out upon them.[29] And it came to pass, when midday was past, and they prophesied until the time of the offering of the evening sacrifice, that there was neither voice, nor any to answer, nor any that regarded.[30] And Elijah said unto all the people, Come near unto me. And all the people came near unto him. And he repaired the altar of the LORD that was broken down.[31] And Elijah took twelve stones, according to the number of the tribes of the sons of Jacob, unto whom the word of the LORD came, saying, Israel shall be thy name:[32] And with the stones he built an altar in the name of the LORD: and he made a trench about the altar, as great as would contain two measures of seed.[33] And he put the wood in order, and cut the bullock in pieces, and laid him on the wood, and said, Fill four barrels with water, and pour it on the burnt sacrifice, and on the wood.[34] And he said, Do it the second time. And they did it the second time. And he said, Do it the third time. And they did it the third time.[35] And the water ran round about the altar; and he filled the trench also with water.[36] And it came to pass at the time of the offering of the evening sacrifice, that Elijah the prophet came near, and said, LORD God of Abraham, Isaac, and of Israel, let it be known this day that thou art God in Israel, and that I am thy servant, and that I have done all these things at thy word.[37] Hear me, O LORD, hear me, that this people may know that thou art the LORD God, and that thou hast turned their heart back again.[38] Then the fire of the LORD fell, and

consumed the burnt sacrifice, and the wood, and the stones, and the dust, and licked up the water
that was in the trench.[39] And when all the people saw it, they fell on their faces: and they said,
The LORD, he is the God; the LORD, he is the God.[40] And Elijah said unto them, Take the prophets of
Baal; let not one of them escape. And they took them: and Elijah brought them down to the brook
Kishon, and slew them there.[41] And Elijah said unto Ahab, Get thee up, eat and drink; for there is a
sound of abundance of rain.[42] So Ahab went up to eat and to drink. And Elijah went up to the top
of Carmel; and he cast himself down upon the earth, and put his face between his knees,[43] And said
to his servant, Go up now, look toward the sea. And he went up, and looked, and said, There is
nothing. And he said, Go again seven times.[44] And it came to pass at the seventh time, that he said,
Behold, there ariseth a little cloud out of the sea, like a man's hand. And he said, Go up, say unto
Ahab, Prepare thy chariot, and get thee down that the rain stop thee not.[45] And it came to pass in
the mean while, that the heaven was black with clouds and wind, and there was a great rain. And
Ahab rode, and went to Jezreel.[46] And the hand of the LORD was on Elijah; and he girded up his
loins, and ran before Ahab to the entrance of Jezreel.

1 Corinthians 6:[19] What? know ye not that your body is the temple of the Holy Ghost which is in you, which ye have of God, and ye are not your own?

1 Corinthians 6:[19] What? know ye not that your body is the temple of the Holy Ghost which is in you, which ye have of God, and ye are not your own?

When or where does this story take place?

List the characters:

Important Words

Is there a problem?

What was the plot or main idea?

Why is this story important?

How can knowing this help me?

1 Corinthians 6:[19] What? know ye not that your body is the temple of the Holy Ghost which is in you, which ye have of God, and ye are not your own?

#29 THE PARABLE OF THE TALENTS

Matthew 25:[14] For the kingdom of heaven is as a man travelling into a far country, who
called his own servants, and delivered unto them his goods.[15] And unto one he gave five talents, to
another two, and to another one; to every man according to his several ability; and straightway
took his journey.[16] Then he that had received the five talents went and traded with the same, and
made them other five talents.[17] And likewise he that had received two, he also gained other
two.[18] But he that had received one went and digged in the earth, and hid his lord's money.[19] After
a long time the lord of those servants cometh, and reckoneth with them.[20] And so he that had
received five talents came and brought other five talents, saying, Lord, thou deliveredst unto me
five talents: behold, I have gained beside them five talents more.[21] His lord said unto him, Well
done, thou good and faithful servant: thou hast been faithful over a few things, I will make thee
ruler over many things: enter thou into the joy of thy lord.[22] He also that had received two talents
came and said, Lord, thou deliveredst unto me two talents: behold, I have gained two other talents
beside them.[23] His lord said unto him, Well done, good and faithful servant; thou hast been faithful
over a few things, I will make thee ruler over many things: enter thou into the joy of thy lord.[24] Then
he which had received the one talent came and said, Lord, I knew thee that thou art an hard man,
reaping where thou hast not sown, and gathering where thou hast not strawed:[25] And I was afraid,
and went and hid thy talent in the earth: lo, there thou hast that is thine.[26] His lord answered and
said unto him, Thou wicked and slothful servant, thou knewest that I reap where I sowed not, and
gather where I have not strawed:[27] Thou oughtest therefore to have put my money to the
exchangers, and then at my coming I should have received mine own with usury.[28] Take therefore
the talent from him, and give it unto him which hath ten talents.[29] For unto every one that hath
shall be given, and he shall have abundance: but from him that hath not shall be taken away even
that which he hath.[30] And cast ye the unprofitable servant into outer darkness: there shall be
weeping and gnashing of teeth.

1 Corinthians 6:[19] What? know ye not that your body is the temple of the Holy Ghost which is in you, which ye have of God, and ye are not your own?

1 Corinthians 6:[19] What? know ye not that your body is the temple of the Holy Ghost which is in you, which ye have of God, and ye are not your own?

When or where does this story take place?

List the characters:

Important Words

Is there a problem?

What was the plot or main idea?

Why is this story important?

How can knowing this help me?

30 THE RICH FOOL

Luke 12: 16 And he spake a parable unto them, saying,
The ground of a certain rich man brought forth plentifully: 17 And he thought within himself,
saying, What shall I do, because I have no room where to bestow my fruits?
18 And he said, This will I do: I will pull down my barns, and build greater; and there will I bestow all
my fruits and my goods. 19 And I will say to my soul, Soul, thou hast much goods laid up for many
years; take thine ease, eat, drink, and be merry. 20 But God said unto him, Thou fool, this night thy
soul shall be required of thee: then whose shall those things be, which thou hast provided? 21 So is he
that layeth up treasure for himself, and is not rich toward God.

1 Corinthians 6:19 What? know ye not that your body is the temple of the Holy Ghost which is in you, which ye have of God, and ye are not your own?

When or where does this story take place?

List the characters:

Important Words

Is there a problem?

What was the plot or main idea?

Why is this story important?

How can knowing this help me?

1 Corinthians 6:[19] What? know ye not that your body is the temple of the Holy Ghost which is in you, which ye have of God, and ye are not your own?

31 The Lost Sheep

MatthewMatthew 18: 12 How think ye? if a man have an hundred sheep, and one of them be gone
astray, doth he not leave the ninety and nine, and goeth into the mountains, and seeketh that which is
gone astray? Luke 15: 1 Then drew near unto him all the publicans and sinners for to hear him. 2
And the Pharisees and scribes murmured, saying, This man receiveth sinners, and eateth with them.3
And he spake this parable unto them, saying, 4 What man of you, having an hundred sheep, if he lose
one of them, doth not leave the ninety and nine in the wilderness, and go after that which is lost, until
he find it? 5 And when he hath found it, he layeth it on his shoulders, rejoicing. 6 And when he cometh
home, he calleth together his friends and neighbours, saying unto them, Rejoice with me; for I have
found my sheep which was lost.7 I say unto you, that likewise joy shall be in heaven over one sinner
that repenteth, more than over ninety and nine just persons, which need no repentance. 8 Either what
woman having ten pieces of silver, if she lose one piece, doth not light a candle, and sweep the
house, and seek diligently till she find it?

Bringing Home the Lost Sheep

1 Corinthians 6:[19] What? know ye not that your body is the temple of the Holy Ghost which is in you, which ye have of God, and ye are not your own?

When or where does this story take place?

List the characters:

Important Words

Is there a problem?

What was the plot or main idea?

Why is this story important?

How can knowing this help me?

1 Corinthians 6:[19] What? know ye not that your body is the temple of the Holy Ghost which is in you, which ye have of God, and ye are not your own?

#32 NEW WINE AND OLD BOTTLES

Matthew 9: 17 Neither do men put new wine into old bottles:
else the bottles break, and the wine runneth out, and the bottles perish:
but they put new wine into new bottles, and both are preserved.

Mark 2: 22 And no man putteth new wine into old bottles:
else the new wine doth burst the bottles, and the wine is spilled, and the bottles will be marred:
but new wine must be put into new bottles.

Luke 5: 37 And no man putteth new wine into old bottles;
else the new wine will burst the bottles, and be spilled, and the bottles shall perish.

5:38 But new wine must be put into new bottles; and both are preserved.

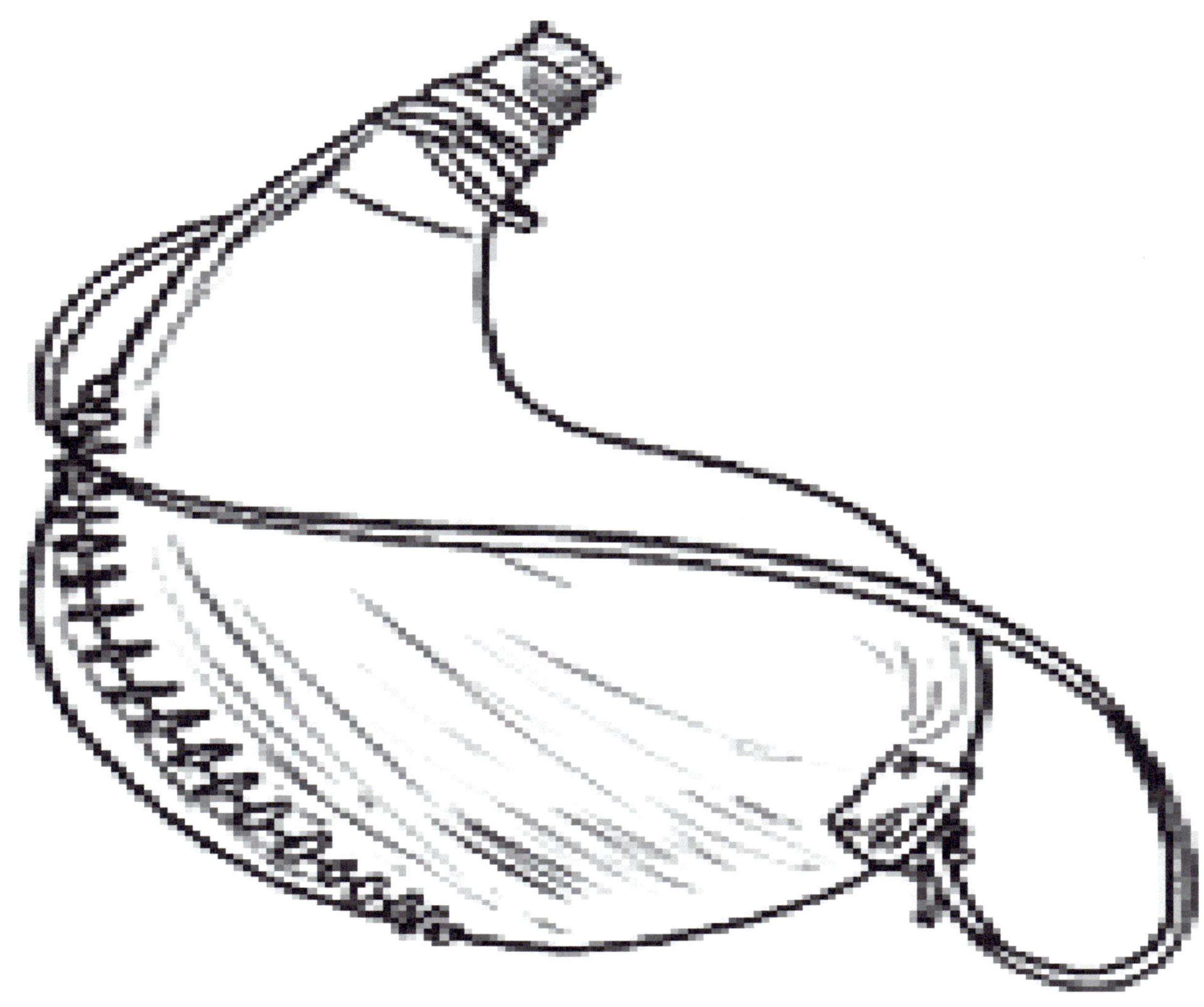

1 Corinthians 6:[19] What? know ye not that your body is the temple of the Holy Ghost which is in you, which ye have of God, and ye are not your own?

When or where does this story take place?

List the characters:

Important Words

Is there a problem?

What was the plot or main idea?

Why is this story important?

How can knowing this help me?

#33 THE SOWER

Luke 8:4 And when much people were gathered together,
and were come to him out of every city, he spake by a parable: 5 A sower went out to sow his
seed: and as he sowed, some fell by the way side;
and it was trodden down, and the fowls of the air devoured it. 6 And some fell upon a rock;
and as soon as it was sprung up, it withered away, because it lacked moisture.
7 And some fell among thorns; and the thorns sprang up with it, and choked it.
8 And other fell on good ground, and sprang up, and bare fruit an hundredfold.
And when he had said these things, he cried, He that hath ears to hear, let him hear. 9 And his
disciples asked him, saying, What might this parable be? 10 And he said,
Unto you it is given to know the mysteries of the kingdom of God:
but to others in parables; that seeing they might not see, and hearing they might not understand. 11
Now the parable is this: The seed is the word of God. 12 Those by the way side are they that
hear; then cometh the devil, and taketh away the word out of their hearts, lest they should believe and
be saved. 13 They on the rock are they, which, when they hear, receive the word with joy; and these
have no root, which for a while believe, and in time of temptation fall away. 14 And that which fell
among thorns are they, which, when they have heard, go forth, and are choked with cares and riches
and pleasures of this life, and bring no fruit to perfection. 15 But that on the good ground are they,
which in an honest and good heart, having heard the word, keep it, and bring forth fruit with patience.
16 No man, when he hath lighted a candle, covereth it with a vessel, or putteth it under a bed; but
setteth it on a candlestick, that they which enter in may see the light.

1 Corinthians 6:[19] What? know ye not that your body is the temple of the Holy Ghost which is in you, which ye have of God, and ye are not your own?

When or where does this story take place?

List the characters:

Important Words

Is there a problem?

What was the plot or main idea?

Why is this story important?

How can knowing this help me?

1 Corinthians 6:[19] What? know ye not that your body is the temple of the Holy Ghost which is in you, which ye have of God, and ye are not your own?

ASSIGNMENT	BOOK OF THE BIBLE	YOUTUBE VIDEO	DATE DUE	DATE COMPLETED

TEACHER SIGN OFF FOR COMPETION CERTIFICATE AT END OF COURSE DATE:______________

1 Corinthians 6:[19] What? know ye not that your body is the temple of the Holy Ghost which is in you, which ye have of God, and ye are not your own?

Notes

1 Corinthians 6:[19] What? know ye not that your body is the temple of the Holy Ghost which is in you, which ye have of God, and ye are not your own?

Notes

Notes

1 Corinthians 6:[19] What? know ye not that your body is the temple of the Holy Ghost which is in you, which ye have of God, and ye are not your own?

Notes

1 Corinthians 6:[19] What? know ye not that your body is the temple of the Holy Ghost which is in you, which ye have of God, and ye are not your own?

Notes

1 Corinthians 6:[19] **What? know ye not that your body is the temple of the Holy Ghost which is in you, which ye have of God, and ye are not your own?**

Notes

1 Corinthians 6:[19] What? know ye not that your body is the temple of the Holy Ghost which is in you, which ye have of God, and ye are not your own?

Notes

1 Corinthians 6:[19] What? know ye not that your body is the temple of the Holy Ghost which is in you, which ye have of God, and ye are not your own?

Notes

1 Corinthians 6:[19] What? know ye not that your body is the temple of the Holy Ghost which is in you, which ye have of God, and ye are not your own?

Notes

1 Corinthians 6:[19] What? know ye not that your body is the temple of the Holy Ghost which is in you, which ye have of God, and ye are not your own?

Notes

Made in the USA
Columbia, SC
03 November 2024

45577251R00076